GETTING TO THE HEART of THINGS

GETTING TO THE HEART of THINGS

Reflections on Christian Basics

MICHAEL CASSIDY

Published by CHRISTIAN ART PUBLISHERS
PO Box 1599, Vereeniging, 1930

© 2005

First edition 2005

Cover designed by Christian Art Publishers

Verses marked NKJV are taken from the New King James Version, copyright © 1979, 1980, 1982 by Thomas Nelson Publishers, Inc. Used by permission.
Verses marked KJV are taken from the King James Version of the Bible.

Set in 11 on 13 pt Palatino BT by Christian Art Publishers

Printed and bound by Interpak Books, KwaZulu-Natal

ISBN 1-86920-582-0

© All rights reserved. No part of this book may be reproduced in any form without permission in writing from the publisher, except in the case of brief quotations embodied in critical articles or reviews.

05   06   07   08   09   10   11   12   13   14   –   10   9   8   7   6   5   4   3   2   1

Dedication

For Bruce Bare and Calvin Cook, two fathers of this work, and for my many other friends and partners in the Gospel on the Boards and Teams of African Enterprise.

Without them, this ministry could never have flourished.

Other Books by Michael Cassidy

The Relationship Tangle
Christianity for the Open-Minded
Bursting the Wineskins
Chasing the Wind
The Passing Summer
The Politics of Love
A Witness For Ever
Window on the Word

Contents

	Preface	9
1.	Questing for the Fundamentals of the Christian Faith	13
2.	Evangelicalism, Liberalism and Fundamentalism	23
3.	Discovering the Bible's View of Itself	30
4.	Biblical Authority as a Corollary of Inspiration	37
5.	Biblical Authority in Church History	46
6.	Interpreting the Bible	55
7.	Mere Christianity for Mere Christians	64
8.	The Uniqueness, Resurrection and Deity of Jesus Christ	72
9.	The Cross as the Real Heart of Things	81
10.	Conversion as the Gateway to Heaven	94
11.	The Person and Work of the Holy Spirit	106
12.	Sanctification	114
13.	Defending and Declaring the Truth	122
14.	Witnessing to an Objective Moral Law	133
15.	Tolerance, Truth and Religious Pluralism	142
16.	A Background to Postmodernism	148
17.	Postmodernism and Post-Everythingism	158
	About the Author	167
	Endnotes	169
	Index	177

Preface

The essays contained in this book are intended to help lay people and pastors to think through the many issues coming headlong at the Christian Church at this convulsive time in our planet's history. In South Africa, and certainly throughout the West, the entrance of the post-Christian or Postmodern era has produced a huge amount of confusion, bewilderment and even loss of nerve amongst many in the Church. Add to this the new and fashionable appeals of religious pluralism and syncretism, interfaith rapprochements, plus New Age spirituality and the Postmodern anathematising of so-called meta-narratives – or universal texts, such as the Bible – and we are facing the development of a right royal crisis among many thinking lay people and clergy. This presents itself in increasing hesitation about evangelism and mission, confusion on Judaeo-Christian ethics and morals, especially in matters of sexuality, plus uncertainty about the uniqueness of Jesus Christ and the concomitant embracing of tolerance as the supreme virtue of our time, which relativises not only morals but truth as well. To be socially, legally, or religiously tolerant, which we salute, is not the same thing as accepting the validity of everything under the sun, whether it is true or not, moral or not, historical or not, factual or not. To do that is to fall perilously prey to the sin of feeble-mindedness and that, surely, can never be the Christian way.

It was this which originally moved me to think about what modest contribution I, as a lay person, could bring within my own circle of contact, in terms of encouraging Christian believers to stand firm on the authority of Scripture, the uniqueness of Jesus, the ongoing importance of mission, evangelism and conversion, the reality of truth as coherence with the facts of life and the universe around us, along with a firm adherence to biblical morality as the way which Jesus Christ as the truth would have us live and behave, if we would have full life in the universe He has made.

There also seemed to me to be a need to underline how we must let the Scriptures speak to the many ethical and moral issues of life and behaviour that face ordinary believers daily. The bulk of that material will come out in a second volume to be entitled *Thinking Things Through*.

All but four of the essays in this book (chapters 9, 10, 16 and 17) were originally sent out with our monthly ministry *Update* newsletter to our African Enterprise mailing list in South Africa as part of a series entitled "Theologically Speaking". They are modest in scope, especially considering the enormity of some of the issues addressed. But many people do not have the time to read vast tomes on these matters and only need a manageable statement setting out the headlines of the issue in a manner both comprehensible and reflective of a genuine attempt to be faithful to the Christian Scriptures. This will often suffice or at least pave the way for any reader desiring to take the matter further with other reading. If this should happen with readers of this present volume, I would feel happily rewarded.

This book (aside from chapters 9 and 10 and the index) first saw the light of day in published form in Australia last year and I am so thankful that Christian Art Publishers are eager now to publish it here in South Africa. I owe a big debt of gratitude to Mike Woodall, director of our African Enterprise office in Sydney, whose vision it originally was to compile my essays and give them a wider readership in book form. My good friend, the Rev. Canon David Hewetson, our African Enterprise Chairman in Australia, ably and judiciously did the initial work of compiling and editing the original essays into a more digestible form. Huge typing labours were put in by Heather Valentine in our Sydney office and I am much indebted to her, as to my former secretary, Colleen Smith, here in South Africa, who typed a number of the original essays. Many thanks to Brenda Harrison, my current secretary, for typing help in the home-straight of the venture, as well as getting the new essays ready for this publication. To Jamie Morrison, my assistant, I am especially indebted for huge labours of proofing and further editing to get these pages finally ready for publication. Thank you also to Rena Pritchard of Acorn Press in Melbourne for all of her work and patience in preparing the essays for their original publication in Australia.

Great gratitude is likewise due to Chris Johnsen and all at Christian Art Publishers for their willingness to venture out on this project here in South Africa and for all their tremendous work in preparing this book for publication.

May these pages bless and encourage all who read them to "contend earnestly for the faith once for all delivered to the saints" (Jude 3).

Michael Cassidy
Pietermaritzburg
August 2005

Chapter One

Questing for the Fundamentals of the Christian Faith

If we are eager to get to the heart of things and to those core, basic and fundamental issues facing Christians today, then we are almost willy-nilly tossed immediately into facing the long-running debate related to three different theological postures or schools of thought known as Evangelicalism, Theological Liberalism, and Fundamentalism.

To reflect on the nature of these postures is not a simple matter of irrelevant semantics and theological hair-splitting. At their heart lies how we use or misuse the Bible, how we interpret or misinterpret it and where, as Christians, we find our locus of spiritual authority. In other words, the debate is about "the fundamentals" of our faith. And it takes us to the very heart of things.

You see, how we read and interpret the Scriptures and how we view their authority or lack thereof is in many ways still a crunch, or crucial issue, as it has been for many centuries. This will determine everything we believe about God and other issues: how we view creation, origins, sin, incarnation, soteriology (i.e., matters of salvation), worship, Church, heaven, hell, conversion, missiology, history, judgement and eschatology (i.e. matters relating to the end of history, the universe and time), how we behave in marriage, the home, sexuality, ethics, morals, money, work, social concern, education, politics, and so on. In fact, every single thing we think, do, or experience in the Christian faith, revolves around how we perceive, understand and use our Bibles.

So, this debate for Christians is not trivial but is about the fundamentals, make no mistake. Entering this arena therefore is not a trifling adventure into the esoteric, but a critically important study of Christian essentials.

It is a quest the Church has been engaged in from the beginning, as when Paul wrote to Timothy to "guard the truth" (2 Timothy 1:14) and to "guard what has been entrusted to you" (1 Timothy 6:20), i.e. the deposit, the content of the Gospel. Jesus Himself prayed that His followers be "sanctified" and "consecrated" in the truth (John 17:17a, 19), adding "thy word is truth" (v. 17b).

Looking back

So let us look back and follow this thread of "guarding Gospel truth" which has always been of much concern to the so-called evangelicals and their forebears, noting Swiss theologian Karl Barth's observation: "We cannot be in the Church without taking as much responsibility for the theology of the past as for the theology of the present."

The battle over "guarding the truth" and the essentials and fundamentals of the faith in our contemporary 20th century era took place within the liberalism-fundamentalism interface in a battle, it seems, which has to be fought afresh in every Church age. Vocabulary, labels, personalities and groups may change, but the perennial challenge remains to establish what it means to "contend earnestly for the faith once for all delivered to the saints" (Jude 3), that is, for the fundamentals of Christianity.

Early Church and Patristic Period

First of all came Jesus, the Apostles and then the early Church. Our New Testament Scriptures and the book of Acts give us a clear account of what they believed, taught and preached as fundamental and essential. Holding to the truth and faith of the Gospel was obviously central in this time. Note Jesus' many corrections of erroneous thought; for example, "you are wrong, because you know neither the Scriptures nor the power of God" (Matthew 22:29). Then there is the whole corpus of Pauline letters, with their omnipresent concern for understanding the Gospel and correctly guarding its truth and keeping it intact.

Next came the Patristic period, the period of the early Church Fathers (AD100-451), the key defining and formative time for the development of Christian fundamentals in doctrine, thought and practice. Great theologians dominated this period, such as Justin Martyr (AD100-165), Irenaeus (AD180), Clement (AD155-c.220), Tertullian (AD160/70-c.215/20), Origen (AD185-c.254), Cyprian (AD200/10-258), Athanasius (AD296-373), and Augustine (AD354-430). During this time, the fundamentals of the faith were enshrined in credal formulae such as the Apostles' Creed (early 3rd century), the Nicene Creed (AD325) and the Definition of Chalcedon (AD435).

Canon

During this period the biblical "canon" of Scripture was also fixed, as the Church reached closure as to which New Testament books carried apostolic imprimatur and belonged in the Bible, and which did not. The Greek word *kanon* speaks of a "rule" or "fixed reference point." With the canon fixed, the Church now had in the New Testament Scriptures 27 books, an authoritative rule or fixed reference point, by which and from which it learned what should rightly be believed and acted upon by Christians.

Quite clearly this was how the issue of scriptural authority appeared in the earliest centuries of the Church's life. It is important to notice that the Church did not confer authority on the Scriptures as if it were a superior authority, but sought merely to discern which texts were either apostolically authored or authorised and therefore, apostolically authoritative. Irenaeus, with Tertullian's strong concurrence, said no text could become Scripture on a par with the Old Testament unless either an Apostle or someone closely connected with them (as with Luke and the author of Hebrews) had written it. Think of it like this: an art specialist does not confer authority or genuineness on a supposed Rembrandt painting, but can only recognise or deny its authenticity. Thus fantastical documents were not included in the canon, while other interesting but not "apostolic" texts (such as those placed in the so-called Apocrypha) were recognised as edifying but denied the weight or authority of Scripture. That understanding is crucial, even today. So in the view of Irenaeus and other early Church fathers, the Church does not create the canon but recognises, receives, preserves and acknowledges the canon God has given to it by His Spirit's work.

While canonical debate on various marginal or disputed texts continued up to early in the 5th century, when the canon was finally closed, in reality the 27 books of our New Testament had already found common acceptance by the end of the 2nd century. Athanasius, Bishop of Alexandria, listed them in AD367. They had proved themselves through quite a long "test of experience" in the Christian community as it experienced the inspiration of the apostolic texts against many fraudulent alternatives. Only in those texts were the essentials and fundamentals of the faith to be found. And in those texts alone was "scriptural" authority to be found.

From the outset, the Church knew itself to be under these Scriptures and that its theology had to be grounded and authorised from there.

Medieval Period

The Middle Ages, which many see as beginning from AD590 when Gregory I became Pope, was a time of mixed fortunes in the Church, when Christian essentials and biblical authority (the issue we are currently following) underwent an assortment of challenges. First of all, although the Roman Catholic Church professed a high view of Scripture, in reality this contained three additional strands: 1) the authority of the Pope, 2) the teaching voice of the Church and 3) Church tradition. All three eventually superimposed themselves on the Bible as the Christian's final authority. With the papacy as a socio-political as well as spiritual power, politics, art, economics and philosophy all became direct concerns of the Church. In many ways, Christianity had accomplished an immense achievement in truly conquering the alien and pagan world of the Roman Empire.

However, the many bright spots aside, there was also much corruption and spiritual declension in the medieval period, as the Church's attempts to control all aspects of life resulted in it overextending itself and becoming secularised at many points in the process. The Church became worldly, even selling "indulgences" by which people could buy supposedly eternal life or release from purgatory for themselves or their deceased relatives. Then in the later Middle Ages, as error and corruption set in, salvation by works and human merit became the erroneous orthodoxy of the day. And of course, while the Scriptures remained in Greek or the Latin Vulgate and therefore inaccessible to the uneducated, the masses languished in ignorance as to what the Bible really taught. Evangelicals, like John Wycliffe in England (1329-1384), Jan Hus in Bohemia (1373-1415) and Girolamo Savonarola in Florence (1452-1498) sought, at the cost of their lives in the cases of Hus and Savonarola, to object to the low, corrupt and unbiblical state of the Church.

Reformation

When Martin Luther (1483-1546) finally nailed his 95 evangelical theses to the door of the Castle Church in Wittenberg, Germany, in 1517, he was lining up with many others sick at heart at the state of things and the loss of both Gospel and Bible in the Church at that time.

At heart again were the issues of authority and the preservation of the essentials and fundamentals of the faith. Thus it was that Luther and the Reformers – such as John Calvin in Geneva (1509-1564), Ulrich Zwingli in Zurich (1485-1531), and William Tyndale in England (1494-1536) – made their celebrated double cry of *sola scriptura* (Scripture alone) and *fide sola* (by faith alone). The first cry was to affirm that the Bible alone is our final authority. The second was that salvation and justification are achieved by grace through faith alone, not works. They upheld these as the two fundamentals of the Christian faith.

The Reformation swept through Europe, with ordinary lay people finally obtaining the Bible in their own languages (German,

French and English) and thus having direct access to its teachings and to the Gospel. The Bible was now becoming re-enthroned at the heart of Christian spirituality. The Reformers, unlike the medieval Roman Catholic priesthood, all believed that to the humble, seeking mind, the Scriptures had a *claritas*, that is, a clarity or perspicuity, by which its basic message and Gospel could be understood without the mediating authority of a priest or professional preacher.

Post-Reformation

Following the Reformation, several other evangelical or pseudo-evangelical movements took centre-stage, each in its own way seeking to grapple with what they saw as Christian fundamentals.

One such movement has been called *Scholasticism* which became problematic because it focussed mainly on faith as doctrinal correctness and the holding of a correct set of evangelical beliefs. As scholars emphasised the place of reason, so theologians, by trying to be more and more "scholastic" and philosophical in their thinking, began to produce a rational, coherent and intellectually defensible system of doctrine. What then occurred unnoticeably, was that "reason" almost replaced personal trust in Christ as saviour and Lord. Some have called this the "period of orthodoxy" (1559-1622).

As Scholasticism became more spiritually arid, two other not-too-dissimilar movements emerged in reaction. The first, called *Pietism*, wanted to see faith relating more fundamentally to personal spirituality and everyday life. People wanted to have their hearts touched, not just to have their heads stuffed with theological data, and so a "feelings" type of spirituality and the warm devotional side of biblical faith were rediscovered. However, said the Pietists, it is all very well to rediscover or affirm biblical authority, but faith should not rest in a doctrine. This movement is epitomised by the famous Count Nicholas Ludwig von Zinzendorf from Moravia (1700-1760), whose followers later helped John Wesley (1703-1791) come to a "born-again" experience in 1738, when Wesley said, "I felt my heart strangely warmed."

Also coming out of the Moravian movement, but going in a slightly different direction from Wesley, was Friedrich Schleiermacher (1768-1834), who also stressed "feeling". For Schleiermacher, the necessary fundamental that affirmed the heart of Christianity rested less in historical facts or divinely revealed truths than in human religious experience. Nevertheless, he too was protesting at barren scholasticism along with those hungry for spiritual reality.

The other significant 17th century movement was *Puritanism*. It further insisted, in the evangelical style, that all questions of faith and morals, including how people lived out their personal lives, be brought to "the touchstone of God's Word." Daily life and Church practices, not just doctrine, had to be reformed. Although much mocked, the Puritans grew rapidly in numbers and in influence. As persecutions mounted, many finally decided to leave Europe for the New World, hoping to find a religious haven where they could express their understanding of faith's fundamentals more freely. These were later to be known as the Pilgrim Fathers and of course they had a profound and determinative effect upon American history, from their 1620 arrival in Massachusetts onwards even up to the present day.

Liberalism

While the Evangelical movements of Pietism and Methodism flourished in Germany and England respectively, and the so-called Great Awakening was capturing many hearts with revival fire in America, the Enlightenment's posture of the 18th and 19th centuries was also gaining ground. Its elevation of Reason, and its enthroning of the scientist over the theologian, challenged all orthodox Christian beliefs, most notably the authority of the Scriptures, the deity and resurrection of Christ, miracles, the virgin birth and Christ's second coming.

American Church historians John Dillenberger and Claude Welch have summarised where things stood as the 19th century opened. They note how the "massive theological systems of the Protestant scholastics, with their concern for precision and subtlety of thought ... had fallen into disrepute", adding: "Their gradual encasing of the vital religious themes of the reformers in a hard shell of doctrines to be believed had meant not only the slow strangulation of the life which those themes expressed, but also the substitution of belief in correct articles of religion for faithful acknowledgment of the living God. And the seemingly endless disputes over theological minutiae had aroused feelings of boredom and disgust. Over against this scholasticism stood a non-religious rationalism which insisted on the full competence of human reason to solve all problems and to offer man effective guidance in life, and which sharply attacked the claims of religion."[1]

This almost secular rationalism and its churchly counterpart in Theological Liberalism demanded that the human characteristics of the Bible be faced, a fair ask. However, because the assumptions and presuppositions were all drawn from secular intellectualism, Christianity and biblical faith began to be radically reworked. Liberal theologians such as Adolf von Harnack (1851-1930) made a massive attack on the Bible and biblical supernaturalism, and also reduced Jesus to a mere man and a great prophet. For Harnack and others, the Christian faith became reduced to three fundamentals: "the universal Fatherhood of God, the infinite worth of the human soul and the law of love for one's fellowmen"[2], an inadequate portrayal.

Also emerging was a socially concerned Christianity (later called the Social Gospel) that stressed ethics at the expense of personal faith and the upliftment of society at the expense of evangelism. Spiritual horizontalism was in, while spiritual verticalism was out, or almost out.

The stage is set

Needless to say, evangelicals (the heirs, as they saw it, of the early Church Fathers and of Luther, Calvin, Wesley, the Pietists and the Puritans) saw this as a drastic assault, diminishing both biblical faith and historical Christianity. Those in America especially felt that it was time to react and reaffirm the essentials, to restate the Fundamentals and recapture biblical authority. Professor T.W.

Manson summarised what they felt: "The attempt of Liberalism to deal with the history of biblical religion was vitiated by its dogmatic presuppositions. Having taken up its axioms, which were at variance with the fundamental ideas of the Bible, there was no way of carrying the business through which did not involve picking and choosing among the biblical material on a scale and with an arbitrariness quite impossible to justify ... All was done with the very best intentions, in the firm belief that Liberalism was on the side of progress, and that the purification and strengthening of the Christian religion was now in full swing. The truth, now coming clearly to light, is that Christianity was being gently and gradually transformed into humanism ... Christianity, in fact, was ceasing to be Christianity."[3]

A Presbyterian scholar, J. Gresham Machen, of Princeton Theological Seminary in New Jersey, wrote: "The liberal attempt at reconciling Christianity with modern science has really relinquished everything distinctive of Christianity, so that what remains is, in essentials, only that same indefinite type of religious aspiration which was in the world before Christianity came on the scene ... the apologist has really abandoned what he started out to defend."[4]

James Packer, an Anglican scholar at Regent College in Vancouver, notes that: "Liberalism swept away entirely the Gospel of the supernatural redemption of sinners by God's sovereign grace. It reduced grace to nature, divine revelation to human reflection, faith in Christ to following his example, and receiving new life to turning over a new leaf; it turned supernatural Christianity into one more form of natural religion, a thin mixture of morals and mysticism."[5]

Reaction

Everywhere, so-called evangelicals reacted, possibly most notably in America where the term "Fundamentalism" was born. In 1910, twelve small volumes entitled *The Fundamentals: A Testimony to the Truth* were published in the United States.

The 65 essays, by 64 significant scholars on both sides of the Atlantic, stressed a series of "fundamentals of the faith". The central ones were:

- The deity of Christ.
- The personality and deity of the Holy Spirit.
- The verbal inspiration of the Bible.
- The virgin birth of Christ.
- His substitutionary atonement.
- His bodily resurrection.
- His imminent and visible second coming.
- The importance of mission and evangelism.

Three million of these volumes were sent at no charge to ministers, evangelists, missionaries, Sunday school superintendents, theological students and the like. The Fundamentalists, as they were soon labelled, had arrived. Theirs was not just a perverse reaction. They were seeking, like their first century counterparts, to "contend for the faith which was once for all delivered to the saints" (Jude 3).

But their quest was not all plain sailing, nor their subsequent history unchequered! In fact it leads into what is still very much a contemporary, current and ongoing struggle, namely, how to establish the exact content of that "faith once for all delivered to the saints", and once established, how to hold it and work it out in grace and truth and love.

And so the old debate is still with us, though in new clothes. That debate we need to explore further. Hopefully it will take us still closer to "the heart of things."

Chapter Two

Evangelicalism, Liberalism and Fundamentalism – An Old Debate with New Clothes

Two of the really bad words around these days, both inside and outside the Church, are "fundamentalist" and "fundamentalism". I wonder sometimes where some political, and indeed Church leaders, would be if they did not have this theological swear-word to toss around (whether they know what it means or not). In fact, once you have labelled someone a "fundamentalist" or more especially a "right-wing fundamentalist" you really do not have to worry about the person anymore. They are discarded, discounted, dead, buried and consigned to the imprisoning box of irrelevance. Categorisation kills them and they no longer matter. They are inconsequential, fundamentalist and we can move on with life!

Recently, when certain Christian activists protested against the new Education Draft Curriculum Proposal in South Africa, the Minister of Education discarded them as "right-wing fundamentalist Christians." That's that, mate! You're dead and we do not even need to consider your views. Likewise a Sunday newspaper declared that those opposed to the proposed curriculum were "critics with fundamentalist leanings." Bang, you're history! Debate closed.

Or, someone in a Church may query whether something is "biblical" or not and be told, "Oh, the trouble with you is that you're too fundamentalist!" Someone I know was chatting with a Church leader about a particular practice, which in his view had no place in a Church service (on this matter, I would have agreed with him), and was told, "You're too fundamentalist." End of story. Finito. No come-back.

I am afraid this kind of thing is often the sad refuge of the uninformed and the unthinking or perhaps, of the insecure.

Can we shed some light on this? In many ways it is confusing, especially when there are Christian people at both ends of the spectrum and in the middle, who say and do things that are very unwise, judgemental and seemingly narrow-minded.

Labels

Although the "fundamentalist" label is often used today to describe radical and extreme Muslims with fanatical political views, such as the September 11th terrorists and the Bali, Madrid and London bombers, here I want to confine myself to the use in Christian circles of the fundamentalist label and as applied to Christian individuals or sectors of the Christian Church.

Let me say first that I believe there are indeed Christians for whom the label is appropriate and it is, in my view, a pejorative label. For myself, I eschew the label, dislike it and reject it, although I do seek to take the Bible and its truth very seriously. Am I therefore a fundamentalist? We need to ask when we can, could or should use the label. And when do we reject it? When is it fair and when unfair? To answer this in these few chapters, we need to look at a little more 19th and 20th century Church history. In doing this, I will also look at a couple of other commonly used labels, even though I basically dislike labels, because they are never neat and exact and often overlap. But two other labels that should be raised here for further reflection are "evangelical" and "liberal", more particularly because so-called "fundamentalism" was born out of a reaction from both of the above: *from* so-called "Evangelicalism" and *to* so-called "Theological Liberalism"!

The initial reaction, in my view, was proper and honourable, but it went wrong and became a corrupted and tragically diminished form of evangelicalism. It led to inappropriate distrust of reason and scholarship, poor apologetics, cultural barrenness, unhelpful individualism, destructive distrust of the wider Church, arrogant exclusivism and chronic judgementalism. All this should alert us to the necessity of extreme care about how and when we use the term "fundamentalism".

Now for the first of these labels. Subsequently, we will look more thoroughly at each of the others.

Evangelical/Evangelicalism

The word "evangelical" comes from "evangel" (meaning Gospel), which in turn comes from the Greek word *euangelion*. This biblical word described the "Gospel" that the early Church preached.

The evangelical faith, therefore, is not a recent development. Indeed, says John Stott, "we dare to claim that evangelical Christianity is original, apostolic, New Testament Christianity."[6] It is also what the Reformers of the 16th century were trying to get back to. Said Martin Luther: "We teach no new thing, but we repeat and establish old things which the apostles and all godly teachers have taught before us."[7] During the English Reformation, Bishop Latimer affirmed: "Ye say it is a new learning. Now I tell you, it is the old learning."[8] In his celebrated *Apology*, John Jewell, Bishop of Salisbury from 1560, affirmed: "It is not our doctrine that we bring you this day; we wrote it not, we found it not out, we are not the inventors of it; we bring you nothing but what the old fathers of the Church, what the apostles, what Christ our Saviour Himself hath brought before us."[9] John Wesley, an evangelical if ever there was one, said: "It is the plain old Christianity which I teach."[10] So the label "evangelical", to which many in today's Church show antipathy, is a noble label with a noble heritage and a long pedigree. John Wycliffe, sometimes called the "Morning Star of the Reformation", was happy to be called "Doctor Evangelicus".

So what do both ancient and modern evangelicals stand for? James Packer lists six basic tenets:

1. The supremacy of Holy Scripture (because of its unique inspiration).

2. The majesty of Jesus Christ (the God-man who died as a sacrifice for sin).
3. The lordship of the Holy Spirit (who exercises a variety of vital ministries).
4. The necessity of conversion (a direct encounter with God effected by God alone).
5. The priority of evangelism (witness being an expression of worship).
6. The importance of fellowship (the Church being essentially a living community of believers).[11]

Another British scholar, David Bebbington, came up with a foursome of "-isms" at the heart of evangelical faith:

1. Conversionism, the belief that lives need to be changed.
2. Activism, the expression of the Gospel in effort.
3. Biblicism, a particular regard for the Bible.
4. Crucicentrism, a stress on the sacrifice of Christ on the cross.[12]

Alister McGrath, of Wycliffe College, Oxford, also has his own summary:

1. A focus, both devotional and theological, on the Person of Jesus Christ, especially His death on the cross.
2. The identification of Scripture as the ultimate authority in matters of spirituality, doctrine and ethics.
3. An emphasis upon conversion or a 'new birth' as a life-changing religious experience.
4. A concern for sharing the faith, especially through evangelism.[13]

John Stott prefers to limit evangelical priorities to a trinitarian threesome:

1. The revealing initiative of God the Father.
2. The redeeming work of God the Son.
3. The transforming ministry of God the Holy Spirit.[14]

I believe that the above cluster of summaries captures what the Church was and has been on about from day one, along with its best theologians, from Clement and Polycarp (AD70-155) to Origen, Tertullian, Augustine, Anselm (1033-1109) and Thomas Aquinas (1224-1274), onwards through Luther and John Calvin to John Knox (1505-1572), Wesley, William Temple (1881-1944) and myriad others. The faith of all these was "evangelical". It is also my faith. That is why I am happy at one level to own the evangelical label. And it lines up with the Apostles' and Nicene creeds. It is, as I see it, the historic faith of the Church when it has been truest to the Gospel. It is enshrined in the Augsburg Confession of the Lutheran Church (1530), the Thirty-Nine Articles of the Anglican Church (1571), and the Westminster Confession of the Presbyterian Church (1646), amongst many other confessional statements. Evangelicalism is not deviationist Christianity. The deviations are elsewhere.

Vigorous debate

The 18th and 19th centuries were a time of vigorous scientific, philosophical and theological debate. It was a time of enormous intellectual vitality and even reorientation of thought. It was the so-called Age of Reason (or Enlightenment), when reason began to prevail over revelation, naturalism over supernaturalism and the scientist over the theologian. Humankind began to put itself over God and to go centre-stage. In all this, there was both a crisis of authority and a flight from authority, as humans declared an ever-increasing autonomy from traditional authorities and from previous faith convictions, including most notions coming from the past. The present and future were "in". The past, with its postures and outdated commitments, was "out". God, the Bible, Jesus, the Resurrection, miracles and faith, all began to be profoundly questioned in the names of our newly omni-competent reason and our newly enthroned scientific enterprise.

Theological Liberalism

Inevitably, theological reflection was profoundly affected by all of this and from that reflection was born a deep and sometimes radical reaction known as Theological Liberalism. It was a very complex movement with many dimensions and degrees, but suffice it for the moment to note that, like most theological movements, it was not totally homogeneous or monolithic. So it had a more conservative component (Evangelical Liberalism) and a more extreme component (Radical Liberalism). The more conservative sector was characterised by a strong, admirable and courageous openness to new information coming from science and philosophy. It sought to mediate and explore the intellectual and theological tensions developing between the new cultural context and the old faith. There was an attempt, sometimes a bit too daring and compromising, to correlate Christian answers with questions raised by increasingly agnostic scientists and philosophers. But this movement was admirable in its intent.

On the other hand, there were the Radical Liberals, ever more powerful, who had little inclination to hold to historic Christianity or cling to "the faith which was once for all delivered to the saints". Their style, like many of their counterparts today, was to accommodate the Christian faith, as fully as possible, to the naturalistic presuppositions and assumptions of "modern culture".

This eviscerated the Gospel, since its theological position, among other things, began increasingly and more extensively to query and deeply challenge the supernaturalism of evangelical faith, including obviously the deity and resurrection of Christ, all miracles and, of course, the authority and inspiration of the Scriptures.

Evangelical reaction

Out of this sweeping movement came, like a swinging pendulum, an intense and vigorous counter-reaction from evangelicals who, in the early 20th century, moved to re-state and re-establish the "Fundamentals of the Faith". This happened between 1909 and

1915, as we said in chapter 1, with the publication of twelve volumes of scholarly essays on the basics of the Christian faith. The authors, though distinguished, and their followers were soon and not surprisingly labelled "fundamentalists".

From then the label stuck, at first honourable and then later derogatory, as a complex and mixed bag history unfolded. But what we need to register is that evangelicals were reacting to what was seen in Liberalism as very theologically compromising. Such perceptions, rightly or wrongly, do produce reactions. And reactions there were and still are.

In fact, finding the proper postures between theological radicalism on the one hand and theological obscurantism on the other is exceedingly difficult.

But suffice it for the moment to caution one and all in dismissing as "fundamentalists" those who seek to take the Bible seriously. The fact is it could make such critics guilty of cheap dismissiveness or even gross misrepresentation. Don't forget John Stuart Mill's dictum: "Misrepresentation is always beautifully brief. Refutation always tediously long."

In any event, the debate being at heart about the Bible, its nature and authority, is incredibly important.

And so to that we now turn.

Chapter Three

Discovering the Bible's View of Itself

Okay! So what it's basically all about is the Bible. In a lot of ways this remains the central battleground in the Christian Church today. What is the nature of the Bible's inspiration and authority? How should we read it, interpret it, receive its teachings, hear its voice and live it out? Yes, that is the key question and the heart of the matter.

That being the case we'll take the next few chapters getting into the inspiration and authority of the Bible for I am convinced that a high view of the Bible and its inspiration is the right one. This has been the historical Christian view until the last 200 years or so and it remains the evangelical view even now. I maintain that this view, for all its difficulties, leaves us in line with Scripture's view of itself, with Jesus' and the Apostles' view of the Old Testament, and with the Apostles' view of their own and each other's writings. In other words, evangelical difficulties are "shared" by both Jesus and the Apostles who both embraced and taught a very high view of scriptural authority and submitted to it themselves.

Theological construct

The evangelical view is essentially a view of faith – a theological construct – based on Scripture's view of itself. If the Bible makes certain express statements about itself – even as it does about the Person of Jesus, or the Atonement, or the way of Salvation, or eschatology or personal discipleship or evangelism – then these statements must take priority in any attempt to form a doctrine of Scripture. Having ascertained Scripture's own self-witness or view of itself, we can then move to the difficulties and apparent contradictions and seek to work through them in the light of this view. We do not move from the difficulties to a view of Scripture, but vice versa. Everett Harrison has noted, "No view of inspiration can indefinitely be sustained if it runs counter to the facts. That the Bible claims inspiration is patent. The problem is to define the nature of that inspiration in the light of the phenomena therein."[15]

Difficulties or apparent contradictions may tempt us to throw over a high view of inspiration and authority, but a faith that is anchored in Jesus will also anchor itself in His view of Scripture and live with any problems this may create. This is preferable, I believe, to abandoning His view and then landing in a sea of subjectivism, relativism and what is often arrogant rationalism. So we do not jettison this view simply because we cannot see how all the problems get resolved. For example, compare any problems you may have regarding the inspiration and authority of Scripture with the problems you might have with how Jesus' humanity and deity coexist. We cannot understand how two natures coexist and fuse in One Person, but we accept it *by faith* on the basis that *He said* that they do. Nor can we grasp or readily reconcile how divine sovereignty and human free will can both be true. So also our problems with the Trinity: Jesus taught a Triune God. Without understanding this, we accept it *by faith* because *He taught it*. So also with Scripture and its divine and human elements. Jesus is therefore the starting point in this, as in all matters of Christian faith.

I believe, therefore, that our steps to a right view of inspiration and authority are as follows:

1. Discover Jesus by coming to the Old Testament and New Testament documents simply and fairly as you would approach any ordinary historical documents. Let the Bible bring us to Christ and to a living faith in Him and experience of Him.
2. Discover Jesus' view of the Old Testament.
3. Discover the Old Testament's view of itself.
4. Discover the Apostles' view of the Old Testament.
5. Discover Jesus' view of His words and their inscripturation.

6. Discover the Apostles' view of their own and each other's writings.
7. Discover the Early Church's view of the New Testament.
8. Discover "the experience" of Scripture.
9. Correlate all the data and seek to formulate a biblical view of scriptural inspiration and authority.

Let's look at these now in more detail.

1. *Discover Jesus.* This is the starting point, the *sine qua non* or indispensable condition of the issue. Take the Old Testament and New Testament text as you would any other and let Jesus reach you. As you would read Caesar's Gallic Wars or Livy's Histories, let the text address you until you find Jesus as your Lord and Saviour. Let the Apostle John's aim in writing his Gospel be fulfilled in you: "These are written that you may believe that Jesus is the Christ, the Son of God, *and that believing you may have life in His name*" (John 20:31). Miss this and we'll miss the rest (See also Section 8, below).

2. *Jesus' view of the Old Testament.* Jesus entered a society already bound by a canon of sacred writings. He never contradicted the prevailing Jewish attitude to the authority of the Law and the Prophets. Indeed He constantly appealed to this corpus of revelation when validating His own Messianic claims. He uses designations such as "Scripture", "the Law", "the Prophets" or "It is written" to refer to the Jewish canonical Scriptures that were held to be sacred and authoritative by all Jews. Furthermore, Jesus equates "God says" with what the text says, as in Matthew 19:4ff. where He quotes the narrator's words in Genesis 2:24 as an utterance of God Himself. Jesus also gives Moses' writings an authority comparable to His own words when, in John 5:45-47, He says, "But if you do not believe his writings, how will you believe My words?" As French theologian Pierre Marcel has said, "From the manner in which Christ quotes Scripture, we find that He recognises and accepts the Old Testament in its entirety as possessing a normative authority, as the true Word of

God, valid for all time."[16] Said Jesus, "Scripture cannot be broken" (John 10:35). Naturally, therefore, error comes when the Scriptures are not properly known or understood. Thus Jesus rebuked the Sadducees, saying, "You are wrong, because you know neither the Scriptures nor the power of God" (Matthew 22:29). These two deficiencies often go together.

3. *The Old Testament's view of itself.* The Old Testament consistently records words that it claims to be God's words. In Genesis 1, for example, this happens ten times. Old Testament writers often say, "And God said" (e.g., Jeremiah 13:15, Amos 3:1, 1 Kings 12:22), a phrase which occurs 3,808 times in the Old Testament. Prophets also claim to be God's spokespersons: "And the Lord said to me, 'Behold, I have put My words in your mouth." (Jeremiah 1:6-9); "The word of the Lord came to me" (Ezekiel 23:1); and "Hear the word of the Lord of hosts" (Isaiah 39:5), etc. Furthermore, God is sometimes said to have written certain words, such as at Sinai (Exodus 31:18, Deuteronomy 10:2) or as instructions for the Temple (1 Chronicles 28:19). Did He write or didn't He? Did He speak or didn't He? Biblical faith says He did!

4. *The Apostles' view of the Old Testament.* Paul, in 2 Timothy 3:16, says that "all Scripture (referring to the Old Testament) is inspired by God". *All*, please note, not *some*. Was Paul right or wrong? If wrong, I'm happy to be wrong with him! In any event we need to note that the word for "inspired" in the Greek is *theopneustos*, meaning "God-breathed", though the meaning is more along the lines of expired than *in*spired. It describes primarily the *manner* in which the scriptural writings originated rather than the *quality* of the finished product. Think perhaps of Beethoven's Ninth Symphony as *inspired* while Scripture is *expired*. We register also that the evangelical claim relates to the manuscripts as originally given and not necessarily as subsequently copied. The possibility of transmission error at a few points cannot be ruled out.

When we read the New Testament, we find that more than ten percent of its text is made up of citations or direct allusions to the Old Testament. In fact, 278 different Old Testament verses are cited in the New Testament, or one verse out of every 22. Not only that, but God is referred to as the author of the Old Testament 56 times in the New Testament. The New Testament writers, like Jesus, often base their argument on only one Old Testament word or even on the grammatical form of one word, as in Galatians 3:16, where Paul's whole thesis rests on the singular form of the word "seed" as opposed to the plural (see Genesis 12:7). The seed, Paul argues, in which the covenant finds consummation, is Christ, singular – an individual – not plural, as referring to a people. This may be Rabbinic exegesis, but Paul is not afraid to use it! The same "single key-word" principle holds true in Matthew 22:44 and John 10:35. In these and other places Jesus' arguments from Scripture rest not upon the general contents but upon a single word or a single letter.

5. *Jesus' view of His own Words and their inscripturation.* In Matthew 24:35, Jesus says that: "Heaven and earth will pass away, but My words will not pass away." He must also have seen that His words would soon become Scripture when, in John 12:48, He says, "the Word that I have spoken will be his judge on the last day." I believe He also had Holy Spirit-inspired inscripturation in mind when He said to His disciples, "When the Spirit of truth comes, He will guide you into all the truth; for He will not speak on His own authority, but whatever He hears He will speak, and He will declare to you the things that are to come. He will glorify me, for He will take what is mine and declare it to you" (John 16:13-14).

6. *The Apostles' view of their own and each others' writings.* Paul sees his own writings as "the word of God" (1 Thessalonians 2:13), as a "command of the Lord" (1 Corinthians 14:37), as revealed (Romans 16:25ff) and as true (Galatians 1:20). Luke sees his writings as orderly, true, accurate (Luke 1:3) and comprehensive (Acts 1:1). John, for his part, sees his writings as thematic, selective, evangelistic (John 20:31) and true (John 21:24-25). It is also fascinating to note that Peter viewed Paul's writings as

"Scripture" (2 Peter 3:16) and also, in some places, as "hard to understand"! Take comfort, fellow strugglers! Then Paul himself quotes both Deuteronomy 25:4 and Luke 10:7 as being "Scripture" in 1 Timothy 5:18. And incidentally, if 1 Timothy was written before Luke, as some think, then Jesus' words in the oral tradition carried the same weight as Scripture.

7. *The Early Church Fathers' view of the New Testament.* Geoffrey Bromiley, an Anglican scholar, has said, "When we turn to the patristic period we are struck at once by the way in which all writers accepted the inspiration and the authority of Holy Scriptures as self-evident."[17] Clement saw the Scriptures as "utterances of this Holy Spirit"[18] while, for Polycarp, a pupil of the Apostle John, the Scriptures were "the voice of the Most High" and "the oracles of God", while those who "perverted them" were seen as "the first born of Satan."[19] Irenaeus in the second century insisted that the Scriptures "were spoken by the Word of God and His Spirit."[20]

8. *The experience of Scripture.* Of course, as we noted earlier, we can have all sorts of head knowledge about the Bible, as well as textual criticism and even theology, but if we have no living new-birth experience of Jesus, the Scriptures will never truly impact us as "the Word of God". My old professor at Fuller Seminary, the great Edward Carnell, once said, "Orthodoxy has always insisted that the written Word does not commend itself as such unless the heart is confronted by the Living Word. Paul did not see Christ in Scripture until he met Christ on the Damascus Road. The Bible does not address the heart as the Word of God until Christ is met in personal fellowship."[21] As I said at the start, this is the essential key. German theologian Helmut Thielicke says the unbelieving theologian can even produce what he calls "diabolical theology". I have seen it and maybe you have too. In fact, whether theology is "sacred or diabolical", "depends", says Thielicke "on the hands and heart which further it."[22]

9. *Correlation of data.* In processing what we learn in evaluating these converging lines of evidence on Scripture's view of itself, we must be careful, therefore, to do it:

- Sacredly, in a spirit of reverence.
- Honestly, following the facts where they lead.
- Humbly, keeping Jesus' authority to the fore.
- Thoroughly, facing the "difficulties" as well.
- Prayerfully, seeking the guidance of the Holy Spirit in all things.
- Charitably, being gracious to those whose conclusions differ from ours, yet not fearing to hold firm to the truth as we understand it.

Chapter Four

Biblical Authority as a Corollary of Inspiration

We underline again that Jesus, the Apostles, the early Church and, indeed, the Church as a whole until the last 200 years, have all had a very high view of the inspiration of Scripture. The last two centuries have seen some in the Church deconstruct this view to such an extent that the Bible becomes just another book with no special qualities to demand that we take it more seriously or accord it more authority than other books, let alone be the sole authority in our lives. But if we do stand with Jesus, the Apostles, the entire Church until the 18th century and the most vibrantly growing portion of the Church today, we can accept that, in the words of James Packer, "What Scripture says, God says. The Bible is inspired in the sense of being (verbally) God-given. It is a record and explanation of divine revelation which is both complete (*sufficient*) and comprehensible (*perspicuous*); that is to say, it contains all that the Church needs to know in this world for its guidance in the way of salvation and service, and it contains the principles for its own interpretation within itself."[23]

As we have seen, Scripture declares itself to be God's Word, with the Old Testament's using, "Thus says the Lord", over 4,000 times. That recurring affirmation, "God spoke", or "God has spoken", calls humankind to hear and heed His voice. Likewise the New Testament writers often speak of "the word of God" for the revelation preserved in the Old Testament. Beyond that, they identify the message of the Gospel as the true meaning of that former

Testament. What they declared was no less authentically the Word of God. When the first Christian believers accepted certain newer writings as Scripture (2 Peter 3:16), it was with the sureness that here too God was speaking. As for Jesus, when faced with the temptations of the devil, He responded to each temptation with, "It is written ... " For Him, what was written in Scripture carried final authority. Can it really be any less for us?

All this shows that our understanding of biblical inspiration must include the notion of it being in at least some sense "verbal" – for we are dealing with "words" which have been written down, or inscripturated. So we can say then that *inspiration* is the term used for the supernatural action of the Spirit of God on the biblical writers. So just as, "By the word of the Lord were the heavens made, and all their host by the breath of His mouth" (Psalm 33:6), so by God's "out-breathing" the Scriptures were produced. As God breathed out life into our first ancestors and they became living souls bearing God's image (Genesis 2:7; 1:27), so God breathed out, through human writers, words that are able to lead us to salvation and instruct us in righteousness, the basic purpose of Scripture, as Paul says to Timothy (2 Timothy 3:16-17).

Not dictation

As well as inspiration being "verbal", we need also to affirm that it is "plenary" – that is, full and complete. This does not mean a "dictation theory" with the human writers passive and not active. In fact it is vital to affirm and reaffirm the double authorship of Scripture – since the Scriptures themselves tell us both that "*God spoke*" (Hebrews 1:1) to and through human writers and that "*men moved by the Holy Spirit spoke from God*" (2 Peter 1:21). John Stott has written: "The Holy Spirit did not obliterate the individual personality of the human authors, any more than their literary style. On the contrary, the Holy Spirit prepared and fashioned the biblical authors (their temperament, genetic inheritance, cultural background, upbringing, education and experience) in such a way as to communicate through each a distinctive and appropriate message."[24]

Stressing that the Bible is both the Word of God and of human beings, he insists we bring both authorships – divine and human – together, and insist that neither contradicts the other.

"On the one hand, the Bible is the Word of God. For God spoke through the human authors in such a way as to determine what He intended to say, yet not in such a way as to violate, let alone smother, the personality of the human authors.

"On the other hand, the Bible is the word of men. For 'men spoke from God' in such a way as to use their faculties freely, yet not in such a way as to distort, let alone destroy, the message of the divine author.

"God spoke His words through their words in such a way that their words were simultaneously His. As a result, what they say God says."[25]

Such double authorship, Stott affirms, demands a double approach. "Because of the kind of book the Bible is, we must approach it in two distinct yet complementary ways. Because it is the Word of God, we must read it as we would read *no* other book – on our knees, in a humble, reverent, prayerful and submissive frame of mind. But because the Bible is also the word of men, we must read it as we would read *every* other book."[26]

This means that we will need to come to the biblical text thoughtfully and with the full application of our mental and spiritual processes.

Authority

The main point of all of this in my view, is not simply to get people holding a particular view of scriptural inspiration, but to get them to submit to its *authority*. That is the key thing. Inspiration needs to make a difference as to how you and I respond to the text, that is, in terms of whether we reject its teachings or submit to them. If indeed the Scriptures are "God-breathed" (*theopneustos* – 2 Timothy 3:16), then as the Westminster Catechism of the Presbyterian Church puts it, "The authority of the Holy Scripture, for which it ought to be believed and obeyed, dependeth not upon the testimony of any man or Church, but wholly upon God (who is truth itself), the author thereof; and therefore it is to be received, because it is the Word of God."

Douglas Johnson, once curator of the British Museum and a top expert in biblical manuscripts, put it this way: "This writer is quite unequivocal in his claim that final authority resides in Holy Scripture solely because it is inspired by God. We are to accept the rule of Scripture over our thoughts because God is its Primary Author. This fact alone gives the Bible its objective authority, and nothing must be allowed to dispute its claim."[27]

Because the Bible claims to be 'inspired' and teaches this about itself, most Christians world-wide accept this, along with the corollary of its consequent authority, even as they accord authority to its teaching on many other things such as the deity of Christ, conversion, redemption, new birth, the work of the Spirit, the importance of mission and evangelism, the Second Coming and so on.

Enlightenment and Postmodernism

However our Postmodern culture, as we will see more fully later, does not respond well to authority. As we will see in our next chapter, when the Reformers and scientists began to question the Church and some of its doctrines in the 16th century and the American and French revolutionaries threw off the monarchy in the 18th, cracks began to appear in the walls of these traditional repositories of authority. Now they are increasingly in danger of crumbling altogether. Not all of the challenges to authority were bad. Many were good and necessary.

If we remove the claimed authority from the Bible, we then have to locate our basic authority internally in Reason or feeling, or conscience and that leaves us drawing in the highly fallible subjective. As we will see, liberal theologians over the last two centuries have heeded the Enlightenment's emphasis on the primary authority of human reason. Others stressed the authority of Church tradition.

More recently, the Postmodern ethos has discarded all so-called Grand Narratives (such as the Bible), as well as all notions of objective or ultimate truth and hence, authority. Each person then, is now his or her own self-styled authority, relying primarily on subjective feelings as a guide to determine what is right and best. Certainly reason, Church tradition and even feelings do have valuable roles to play in our grappling with the meaning of Scripture but ultimately they cannot be the final arbiters of what the truth really is. Only the Holy Spirit can do that for us.

American theologian David Wells puts it this way: "Without this transcendent Word in its life, the Church has no rudder, no compass, no provisions. Without the Word, it has no capacity to stand outside its culture, to detect and wrench itself free from the seductions of modernity. Without the Word, the church has no meaning. It may seek substitutes for meaning in committee work, relief work and various other church activities, but such things cannot fill the role for very long. Cut off from the meaning that God has given, faith cannot offer anything more by way of light in our dark world than what is offered by philosophy, psychology or sociology. Cut off from God's meaning, the church is cut off from God; it loses its identity as the people of God in belief, in practice, in hope. Cut off from God's Word, the church is on its own, left to live for itself, by itself, upon itself. It is never lifted beyond itself, above its culture."[28]

"While the signs of the crisis in the churches proliferate", writes Paul T. Stallsworth, "the reason for the crisis remains constant, the sovereign self, understood apart from the Lordship of Jesus Christ, His Cross, His Church, and His Kingdom [and, he might have added, His word], is taken to be the maker and shaper of the self's nature and destiny."[29]

While we must find new and creative ways to minister to and share the Gospel with people in our increasingly Postmodern culture who do not acknowledge any higher authority than themselves, we cannot surrender in any measure the full and final authority of Scripture. Nor is this just an academic exercise because walking in the Bible's ways brings us joy and fulfilment, while non-Jesus ways do not work and only bring us frustration and sadness. In other words, the Bible is God's authoritative and highly practical guidebook and believing it or disbelieving it has profound implications for what we believe, where we find salvation and how we behave.

That's why we should take it seriously, very seriously.

We should believe it

Thus, for example, if the Bible says, "You must be born anew" (John 3:3), we should believe it, not dismiss it. Moreover, if it says that without the new birth we will neither "see" (John 3:3), let alone "enter the Kingdom of God" (John 3:5), we should believe it, for eternal destinies are at stake. If the Scriptures say that Jesus is "the way, and the truth, and the life" (John 14:6a) and that "no one comes to the Father, but by me" (John 14:6b), we should believe it, not evade it. If John's Gospel says that, "He who believes in Him (Jesus) is not condemned; he who does not believe is condemned already, because he has not believed in the name of the only Son of God" (John 3:18), then it is eternal folly to ignore such a word. Likewise the equally startling word at the end of that chapter, "He who believes in the Son has eternal life; he who does not obey the Son shall not see life, but the wrath of God rests upon him" (v. 36). Modern people and even many Church leaders, totally reject the idea of the wrath of God and wallow in a sentimental view of His love. The Bible speaks otherwise. To ignore this is to betray the authority of Scripture. So too, we must undoubtedly feel a profound challenge when Jesus speaks of that Final Day when some will ask, "'Lord, when did we see you hungry or thirsty or a stranger or naked or sick or in prison, and did not minister to you?' Then He will answer them, 'Truly, I say to you, as you did it not to one of the least of these, you did it not to Me.' And they will go away into eternal punishment, but the righteous into eternal life" (Matthew 25:44-46). Is that true or not true? If we take the inspiration and authority of Scripture seriously, we will say it is true. This is not to say that we disregard sound hermeneutical principles (more on this later) in our reading of the Bible but, as I have said previously, we can trust (with the Reformers) in the "*claritas*" (Latin for clarity, or understandability) of the Scriptures and seek to take them at face value.

Thus, when Jesus speaks of "murder, adultery, fornication, theft, false witness, slander" as "evil" (Matthew 15:19), He means just that. They are evil. They are not okay. In a similar vein, the Bible says, "You will not have intercourse with a man as you would with a woman. This is a hateful thing." (Leviticus 18:22) This clear admonition is in line with the description in Genesis 1 and 2 of God's creation of man and woman as being physically and sexually complementary to one another, as well as with Paul's lament that "the men ... gave up natural relations with women and were consumed with passion for one another, men committing shameful acts with men and receiving in their persons the due penalty for their error" (Romans 1:27).

Many these days want to see in Scripture a sanction for – or at least an absence of hostility toward – homosexual behaviour. But what the Bible says on this is as clear as the sun on a cloudless day at noon. It sees such behaviour as "shameful", and "unnatural", i.e. contrary to nature (Romans 1:26-27) though requiring our compassionate response. So if the Bible is manifestly clear on this issue, we must take God at His word and submit to the authority of Scripture rather than to the morally relaxed and accommodating spirit of the age.

So, too, when all four Gospels and the Ascension story in Acts 1 give us Jesus' Great Commission – the evangelisation of the world as His final injunction to His disciples – we can hardly evade or avoid being busy with evangelism. In other words, if we take Scripture seriously, His last command has to become our first concern.

The real issue

My own view on all this is that the real issue under review lies not so much in what precise definition we have of scriptural inspiration, but rather in whether we will really take the Bible seriously or not. If we do not, we can only flounder in evangelistic paralysis, ethical relativism and human guesswork on both doctrine and behaviour. Both the Church corporately and each of us individually will be far better served if we follow three expedients:

1. *We must heed the instructions of the whole Bible, not just favourite portions.* The Bible in its entirety is God's message and progres-

sive revelation to us. To receive this aright we need to immerse ourselves in the Scriptures because they have important things to say to us. We should also remember Jesus saying, "For truly, I say to you, till heaven and earth pass away, not an iota, not a dot, will pass from the Law until all is accomplished" (Matthew 5:18).

2. *We must acknowledge our need to conform our behaviour to Scripture's ethics and ways.* When we are challenged or confronted by the Scriptures, we can be sure that God is speaking to us in order to get us to change our attitudes or behaviour for our own good as well as for His glory. Of course this is often very difficult for us, but the challenge stands and is to be taken seriously.

3. *When faced with difficulties or mysteries in the text, we must not reject the Bible's inspiration or authority*, as taught by Scripture itself, but work and study in integrity to find the best way through. In this, as Rev. Peter Mason said at the *Anglican Essentials* Conference in Toronto in June 1994, we will indeed "use our God-given reason to the best of our ability but we will also recognise its finiteness and fallibility and therefore submit to God's Word at those crucial points where our logical conclusions seem at variance with it. Furthermore, we humbly test our individual understandings and interpretations of Scripture with the insights of the wider community, the Church, drawing upon the wisdom of scholars, commentators, wise and godly mentors, and all those whose Christian experience qualifies them to help us discern God's truth and God's will."[30]

Key challenge

Mason is also helpful when he adds that the key challenge is *submission* – that is, heeding "the call to the whole Church, and indeed to humankind in its entirety, to bring every thought, every value, every decision, every action into conformity with the will of God as it is disclosed in Scripture ... The biblical vocation is to make Jesus Christ known, trusted, obeyed, and glorified by each and every human being who owes his or her very existence to the one great God of the universe and to whom accountability will ultimately still be given by one and all."[31]

He concludes, "Today more than ever, individual Christians, and every church congregation, diocese, and denomination, must recapture confidence in the truthfulness, reliability, and power of Scripture, to save, renew, and prepare women and men for life in God's kingdom, now and in the age to come."[32]

5

Chapter Five

Biblical Authority in Church History

As we've seen in our previous few chapters, when we look at Scripture from the viewpoint of Jesus, the Apostles and the early Church, we find that they all had an extremely high view of the Bible and of its inspiration and consequent authority. Thus, if we also hold a high view of Scripture, we know that we are in good company in sharing their view, even if there are "difficulties" to be worked through viewing Scripture in this way. But not everyone today, even within the Church, has such reverence for the Bible. What has happened in the past 2,000 years?

Early Church and Patristic Period

When we look back over the history of the Church, we find that the inspiration and authority of the Bible has really only come to be seriously questioned in the last 200 years. The early Church, as indicated, but I must underline it, had tremendous respect for Scripture. During the Patristic period from AD100-400, for example, Origen believed that "the Holy Spirit was co-worker with the evangelists in the composition of the Gospel so that lapse of memory, error or falsehood was impossible for them."

For him "the sacred volumes are fully inspired by the Holy Spirit and there is no passage either in the Law or the Gospel, or the writings of an Apostle, which does not proceed from the inspired source of Divine Truth."[33]

With that posture Polycarp, Irenaeus, Tertullian, Cyprian, Clement would all have agreed. For Athanasius, a fourth-century father, "The Holy Scripture is mightier than all synods ... The whole of our Scriptures, the Old Testament and the New Testament, are profitable for instruction as it is written." To him the Bible is "a Book wholly inspired by God from beginning to end." He even said that "each Psalm has been spoken and composed by the Holy Spirit."[34]

And for his part Augustine asserted that: "The faith will totter if the authority of Holy Scripture loses its hold on men. We must surrender ourselves to the authority of Holy Scripture, for it can neither mislead or be misled."[35]

However, some of the Patristics introduced the notion that the Scriptures were "dictated" to the biblical writers by God, an idea which opened the way to a rigid, mechanical view of inspiration and tended to eliminate the principles both of the Holy Spirit's illumination of the reader and of His not obliterating the human makeup of the writers. This created the potential for placing a greater emphasis on the letter than on the spirit of the law.

Middle Ages

As the Church began to become more institutionalised, the status of the Bible became defined in relation to other authorities in the Church, most notably the Pope. The emphasis then was placed on the Church as the interpreting authority of Scripture. Thus the Pope, Church tradition and the Bible were authoritative, in that order. There were of course problems with this situation because the Bible was not in the language or the hands of the common people. They were scarcely allowed to read the Scripture, nor were they able to. They were therefore unable to check or question the interpretations, judgements and even abuses by the Church authorities. Nevertheless, the issue of hermeneutics (the science of interpretation) was beginning to appear, since it was obviously necessary for Scripture to be interpreted. "What did the Bible say? What did the Bible mean?" were two questions constantly before the Church.

During this period of the Middle Ages, the extraordinarily high and even rigid view of Scripture that the Patristics maintained, came to be adjusted somewhat by some of the thinkers of the period. One such person was Thomas Aquinas. He believed that the Holy Spirit was the true author of the Bible but that He did not in any way overrule the human authors.

Reformation

Because the Church in the Middle Ages set itself up as the sole interpreter of Scripture, it inevitably began to abuse the Scriptures and instituted questionable practices. In the 16th century Reformation period, some within the Church – most notably Luther in Germany, Calvin and Zwingli in Switzerland and Tyndale in England – questioned and opposed these abuses. While calling the authority of the Church into question however, Luther and the other Reformers still took a very high view of the inspiration of Scripture for granted. Luther said the whole Bible must be accepted as the inspired Word of God. John Calvin adds: We owe to the Bible "the same reverence which we owe to God because it has proceeded from Him alone." Indeed "We ought to embrace with mild docility, and without exception, whatever is delivered in the Holy Scriptures. For Scripture is the school of the Holy Spirit in which as nothing useful and necessary is omitted, so nothing is taught which is not profitable to know."[36]

The Reformers emphasised Christ as the main theme of the Bible and that the purpose of Scripture was to try to bring people to Him. They also emphasised the human aspects of the Bible in conjunction with the divine; that is, the divine message was given in and through the human experience. One of the most important things the Reformers did was to translate the Bible into the language of the common person so that everyone could have a Bible and read it in their own language. Thus, Luther translated the Scriptures into German, Calvin into French and Tyndale into English.

With the Bible now in the language and the hands of ordinary people, the Reformers stressed that the Holy Spirit must illuminate the mind of the reader. Said Luther: "The Bible cannot be mastered by study or talent; you must rely solely on the influx of the Spirit."[37] And Whittaker, an Anglican Reformer said, "The Holy Spirit is the supreme interpreter of Scripture, because we must be illuminated by the Holy Spirit to be certainly persuaded of the true sense of Scripture."[38]

While the Reformers ultimately split off from the Roman Catholic Church, the Roman Church stated at its Council of Trent that, "God is the author of Scripture." The Reformers did not differ from Rome on the inspiration of Scripture but on its authority, with the Roman Church continuing to give greater authority to the Pope and to the tradition of the Church. But Article VI of the Thirty-nine Articles of the Church of England said, "Holy Scripture containeth all things necessary to salvation, so that whatsoever is not read therein, nor may be proved thereby, is not to be required of any man, that it should be believed as an article of the Faith, or be thought requisite or necessary to salvation. In the name of the Holy Scripture we do understand those Canonical Books of the Old and New Testament, *of whose authority was never any doubt in the Church*" (italics added).

While the Reformers did hold an extremely high view of Scripture, they nevertheless had dared to question the authority of the Pope and of the Roman Church, something that had not been done successfully for 1,500 years. And they were not the only ones to do this. Copernicus and Galileo challenged the Church's teaching that the earth was at the centre of the universe, and of course they were proved right. Not only was the Church successfully challenged during this time, other authorities were dispensed with as well. The American colonies went to war against Britain from 1775-81 and gained their freedom to determine their own destiny. And in 1789, the French people revolted against the authority of their monarchy and aristocracy.

Eighteenth Century Enlightenment

Since the Church and the monarchical state had for so long been the arbiters of what was true and right in society, in the questioning or even sometimes stripping of their authority, something else had to take their place. This something was Reason, the essential characteristic of the 18th century Enlightenment. People began to have confidence in themselves as capable of determining what was true, rather than looking to some external authority to determine it for them. A typical watchword of the Enlightenment was *sapere aude*, or "have the courage to make use of your own understanding." This spirit inevitably spilled over into the world of theology. Religious people began to argue that they had by dint of reason, the power to understand the world around them. And if this was so, it meant they had to be so in accord with the God who had created the world, that there was an essential oneness and harmony between their reason and God's. It was assumed that God had said "Yes" to people as they were, with their reason as it was. Believing that human reason was an extension of God's reason, people began to accept from the Bible *only those things which were not offensive to human reason* and which agreed with the idea of a harmony between people and God.

Ideas like human depravity, new birth, redemption through the blood of Christ and justification by faith were increasingly discarded. Being essentially divine, people had no need of all this. The idea that human reason could also be fallen, rebellious and subject to sin was not in purview. The notion of intellectual as well as volitional repentance seemed unthinkable.

Nineteenth Century

Out of the Enlightenment flowed religious liberalism which flourished in Europe from about 1860 to the early 1900s and to which we alluded to in chapter 2. This movement, with many admirable features (for example, its generosity of spirit and adventurous intellectualism), was dominated by:

- Tolerance.
- Respect for science and the scientific method (F.D. Maurice).
- Tentativeness or scepticism of achieving certain knowledge of ultimate reality.
- Confidence in "man, his dignity and his future."
- God's immanence or closeness.
- Religious experience (Schleiermacher and Ritschl).
- The humanity of Jesus (who was often seen as no more than a

man), and who asks for "no belief in Him other than obedience to His teachings" (Harnack).

Religious authority now became invested in religious experience, not in the so-called "finite authorities of Bible, Church or tradition." Historians Dillenberger and Welch write: "The final court of appeal becomes one's own reason, conscience, and intuition. The witness of the Scriptures, of the creeds and traditions of the Church and of the existing Christian community, becomes subordinate to one's individual religious insight."[39]

It was also said by some (e.g. Ernest Troeltsch) that neither Jesus nor Christianity, but the human spirit as a whole, represented by all the great religious lights, should be the norm for Truth. Thus did the liberal spirit, biblical criticism, the accompanying abandonment of the verbal inspiration of the Bible, a new social concern, full recognition of the humanity of Jesus and humanistic optimism begin to hold sway as the 20th century opened.

Twentieth Century

However, the world's optimism and liberalism's subjectivism and confidence in human beings were severely shaken as World War I, with its rampant evil, broke out. In accordance with the prevailing philosophy of liberalism, with its confidence in people *as they are* as a part of the divine, there was no *objective norm* available to prevent 93 German intellectuals, including Harnack and a number of other liberal theologians, from signing a petition in 1914 which approved of Kaiser Wilhelm II's policies. These included shooting civilians and children in his march across Belgium and the burning of the library at Louvain with its irreplaceable treasures. The fact that Harnack and other liberal theologians signed this petition had enormous implications for theology, for it produced a theological rebellion. The modern theological debate in fact, is all part of a reaction against 19th century liberalism and its presuppositions. Three men – Karl Barth, Oscar Cullmann and Rudolph Bultmann – have been the ones largely responsible for shaping this reaction, with the Bible as the central battleground. While the three all reacted against liberalism, they did not agree as to what exactly should take its place. They each wanted to understand New Testament faith as that which confronts humankind from without, but they differed regarding the presuppositions by which one should come to understand this New Testament faith.

Karl Barth (1886-1968)

When Barth, then a young Swiss pastor, saw the petition containing the signatures of many of his former theological teachers, he decided something was radically wrong with theological liberalism. He went back to Scripture, and especially to Paul's letter to the Romans, where he came to the devastating conclusion that God and His reason were not in accord with humans and their reason. Barth saw scriptural revelation centred in Christ. But he asserted that the Scriptures are not in and of themselves a revelation from God, as "a witness is not absolutely identical with that to which it witnesses." The Bible then according to Barth is not the Word of God, but *contains* the Word of God. Put differently, parts of the Bible become the Word of God to me in personal encounter as I meet the living Christ through them. One does not therefore reason one's way objectively through to what the Word of God is saying. One is simply confronted by Jesus as the Living Word in personal encounter.

Oscar Cullmann (1902-1999)

If Barth saw all revelation as subsumed in Christ, Cullmann believed that revelation does not remain identical with Jesus, but also exists in the very words of Scripture. Since revelation has become history, the events of redemptive history become "facts which are the object of faith." In coming to grips with Scripture's relating of these facts, Cullmann stressed, we must try to avoid superimposing on it the ideas of the 20th century. We must listen to what the Bible itself wants to say and not to what some moderns would like it to say.

Rudolph Bultmann (1884-1976)

Bultmann's system of interpretation, on the other hand, was based on his conviction that people find a mysterious discontent within themselves, i.e. they are not content to be. Rather there is within us an imperative decree to live *responsibly*, or what Bultmann called "authentically". He saw this as an intuitive knowledge possessed by every person. It is this knowledge which provides the basis for interpreting the Bible. Thus Bultmann's hermeneutical principle is to *let human reason decide what constitutes authentic living*, which in its turn decides in advance what is valid in the New Testament and what must be re-interpreted. Bultmann's presuppositions were again basically naturalistic.

C.S. Lewis (1898-1963)

C.S. Lewis, for his part, was very critical of the way much modern textual criticism of the Bible is indeed rooted in the naturalistic presuppositions of many biblical critics. Thus can he note that "scholars as scholars cannot speak on the supernaturalism of the text with more authority than anyone else." He adds that their naturalistic presupposition – if it's miraculous, then it's not historical – "is one they bring to their study of the texts, not one they have learned from it.

If one is speaking of authority, the united authority of all biblical critics in the world counts here for nothing. On this they speak simply as men, men obviously influenced by, and perhaps insufficiently critical of the spirit of the age they grew up in."[40] Lewis also laments the fact that, "the undermining of the old orthodoxy has been mainly the work of divines engaged in New Testament criticism. The authority of experts in that discipline is the authority in deference to whom we are asked to give up a huge mass of beliefs shared in common by the early Church, the Fathers, the Middle Ages, the Reformers and even the 19th century."[41] He, for one, refused to do that.

We see then that it was basically the 18th century's exaltation of human reason which launched the overthrow of biblical inspiration and authority in many parts of the Church in the 19th and 20th centuries and resulted finally in the pitiful confusion we see now in many sectors of the Church. With biblical authority and inspiration set aside, many no longer know what the Christian message (*kerygma*) is by which people "may be saved" (1 Corinthians 1:21). Nor does it matter much, seeing that salvation as historically understood is for many not necessary. Thus are the nerve and know-how of the evangelistic imperative lost and traditional Christian ethics left in disarray. Instead, the Church's exclusive work, backed by a theology often at the end of its tether, becomes simply to be involved in social action, in working for peace and in fighting against disease. All of which is vital, but it is hardly the whole requirement of the Gospel.

Thankfully there were more conservative scholars and thinkers, even from the beginning of the last century, who, like Lewis later on, refused to kowtow to the liberal assault on Scripture and who held to the traditional view of biblical inspiration and a high view of biblical authority.

Thankfully too, from their strong stance (which has also had its own inevitable problems and weaknesses), came ultimately the evangelical, charismatic and Pentecostal resurgence of the 20th century – these being the major sectors of the Church where there is still significant and consistent growth and major evangelistic ministry. However, there is something else to note. This is that sometimes the divisions or gaps come, not because one lot of people affirm the Bible's authority, while another lot denies it, but because people who all claim to accept the Bible's authority nevertheless interpret its text and contents differently.

So to this issue of biblical interpretation we need now to turn.

Chapter Six

Interpreting the Bible – Some Thoughts on Hermeneutics for Today

This big word "hermeneutics" is one theologians use to describe the science and discipline of interpreting the Bible.

Today this issue is on the table in new ways and with new vigour. In fact, in many ways our struggles relating to religious pluralism, syncretism, universalism (the doctrine that everyone will ultimately be saved) plus ethical issues such as abortion, homosexuality, biblical sex ethics or even whether we should evangelise, revolve in some way around this matter of biblical interpretation, for it affects all arenas of doctrine and life, including the very witness itself of the Church to the world.

It is well known that varying views have been espoused on the subject of scriptural inspiration, none without its difficulties. As indicated clearly already, I personally believe a high view of the Bible and its inspiration is the right one. Though not all Christians today would accept the evangelical understanding of Scripture, as we've noted, it remains by and large the historical Christian view and was not questioned seriously until the so-called Enlightenment of the 18th century.

A high view of the Bible, however, does not allow us to be cavalier in our treatment of the text or make it support eccentric notions by the loose and erratic use of proof texts, which Paul describes as "tampering with God's Word" and "twisting it" to suit people's own private purposes (2 Corinthians 4:2; 2 Peter 3:16). It is important to avoid giving any validity to the critic who would say, "You are just twisting the Bible to make it mean anything you like." The hard fact is that we *can* make the Bible mean just about anything we like if we are unscrupulous with it. But if we are scrupulously honest and humble in our approach to the text and in our use of sound principles of interpretation, we will not manipulate the Scriptures but find ourselves controlled and directed by them.

And certainly we will not allow ourselves to succumb to "bibliolatry", or the worship of the Bible itself. We are to worship God. But the written Word is intended to lead us to the Living God and to a life of love and service.

What does it say and mean?

However, when we receive the Bible as inspired and authoritative, two questions remain:

1. What is it saying?
2. What does it mean?

First, each reader of Scripture must guard him or herself against pretending or claiming that any of us can personally have an infallible understanding of Scripture. While God's Word is wholly reliable and authoritative, some of our interpretations may not be. Indeed, one could go further and say that no individual, no group, Church or denomination has ever been or will ever be an infallible interpreter of God's Word. However, different Christian groupings often create from their own interpretation of the text strong traditions to which they ascribe something akin to infallibility, even when these are at variance with each other! The fact is that even our most cherished Christian traditions must constantly be judged at the bar of Scripture.

As we do so, we will register afresh that God has indeed made provision for us to grow in our understanding of the truth and to be protected from the worst forms of misinterpretation.

We must also note that none of us comes to the biblical text with minds that are *tabula rasa*, that is, as a clean slate. We all have experiences and upbringings and conditionings which make us receive certain facets of Scripture and disregard others. In a sense we each have our own pre-understandings or "hermeneutical grid" – shaped by many factors – through which we filter the text. Our psychological, intellectual and biographical make-up is such that it is extremely difficult for us to be changed by a text or to have our own thought processes and preconceived ideas rearranged by what comes to us in the text. That's why it is important sometimes to have our interpretations adjusted by others' interpretations because understandings which are born out of fellowship rather than isolation, are more likely to be correct.

Principles of interpretation

As we approach the Bible, we must also recognise that we are separated by several types of gaps between the text and us, all of which require for us some clear rules for interpretation. There is the double horizon of the text itself in its original setting, and ours in our own setting. But the key principle to follow, I believe, is that of the normal grammatico-historical approach used on any text. In other words, we first apply basic rules of grammar both to the text and to the historical context in which it was birthed and authored. We are to let the text speak and then seek the meaning of the verse or passage by taking into account and examining the following:

- *Literary form*: Is the passage history, poetry, allegory, parable, doctrine, prophecy etc.?
- *Historical context*: What did it mean to those who first heard it in their contemporary contexts?
- *Cultural context*: What were the cultural understandings that would influence the original readers, and which might or might not pertain to us now?
- *Linguistic meaning*: What is the meaning or nuance of a word or passage in the language in which it was originally written? Comparison of word usage is critical.
- *Grammatical sense*: What is the plain, obvious, literal, natural and customary grammatical sense of a word or phrase?

Progressive revelation

With this basic approach in place and accepting the inspired unity of the Bible, we need also to recognise the reality of God's progressive revelation in the biblical Scriptures. In other words God did not reveal His whole mind, will and purpose at the beginning of the Bible. His light and mind were revealed gradually and progressively as the human race generally, and His chosen people, the Jews specifically, were ready to receive them. Clearly when the human race was totally primitive, God had to deal with people as He found them, many of their mores and customs being crude, basic and defective. So each stage of divine revelation has to be interpreted by us from within the spiritual and cultural developmental stage of the people being addressed. Clearly in Moses' and then Solomon's time polygamy was accepted, but when Jesus came He said monogamy was the highest divine way. The Psalmist likewise called down destruction on his enemies, which no Christian in the light of Jesus' teaching could emulate.

Again, Jesus' standards relating to divorce were much higher than those of Moses. In the Old Testament the divide between Jew and Gentile was not only allowed but effectively mandated. In the New Testament, Jesus says that was for then. It is not for now. Even the disciples battled with this.

So we interpret the lower stages in the light of the higher with corrective understandings which come with the higher.

Says Edward John Carnell, one of my former professors at Fuller Seminary: "Two principles must be kept in delicate balance: *first*, the whole of Scripture is inspired; *secondly*, some parts of Scripture are subject to the illumination of other parts. If a Christian neglects the second principle, out of a zeal to honour the first, his conduct hardly conduces to healthy Biblical faith."[42]

Carnell also affirmed a logical hermeneutical process, which I always found incredibly helpful:

1. The New Testament interprets the Old Testament.
2. The Epistles interpret the Gospels.
3. Systematic passages interpret incidental ones.

4. The universal interprets the local.
5. Didactic and teaching passages interpret symbolic passages.
6. The clear interprets the obscure.
7. Scripture interprets Scripture.[43]

Let's look at these now in greater detail.

1. *The New Testament interprets the Old Testament.* The writer to the Hebrews tells us the Old Testament is a shadow (Hebrews 10:1), while the New Testament is the Real Thing. Old Timers used to say that the New Testament is latent in the Old Testament, and the Old Testament patent in the New. Old Testament prophets anticipated the Messiah. The Apostles saw Him face to face. So the Old Testament cannot have a primary place in our thinking over and above the New Testament. The former anticipates. The latter fulfils. So the New Testament interprets the Old.

2. *The Epistles interpret the Gospels.* Jesus told His disciples that: "I have yet many things to say to you, but you cannot bear them now. When the Spirit of truth comes, He will guide you into all truth." (John 16:12-13) Clearly Jesus anticipated that after the Gospel accounts of His earthly life, more truth would come. In this He was surely anticipating the Epistles. The Gospels begin our teaching on the Holy Spirit (e.g. John 16). The Epistles complete the task (e.g. 1 Corinthians 12 and 14). Likewise, when Jesus was asked what "works" were the work of God, He declared in brief the principle of Justification by Faith ("This is the work of God that you believe in Him whom He sent" – John 6:29). But it was left to the Apostle Paul to interpret this out fully in Romans, Galatians, Ephesians, Titus, etc. The Epistles interpret the Gospels.

3. *Systematic passages interpret incidental ones.* Thinking again of justification by faith, we note that in Romans and Galatians, Paul treats this in an elaborate, systematic and extended way. So while justification by faith is implied or referred to incidentally or in passing all over the New Testament, only in Romans

and Galatians is it spelled out fully. So the full, didactic, and theological passages must interpret those passages where the reference is incidental or very brief.

4. *The universal interprets the local.* It was a custom in first-century Palestine, with its sand and sandals, to wash the feet of a guest or friend. And Jesus did it for His disciples to demonstrate love and humility. The universal principle is love and humility. The local custom and vehicle then was foot-washing. Today we retain the universal principle while normally dispensing with the local first-century custom. The universal interprets the local.

5. *Didactic and teaching passages interpret symbolic passages.* In Matthew 24 and in books such as 1 and 2 Thessalonians, Jesus and the Apostle talk and teach much about the Second Coming of Christ. It is these open and relatively plain passages which in broad terms must provide the key clues to understanding and interpreting the highly symbolic and mysterious passages on this subject which come in the Book of Revelation, or the Book of Daniel.

6. *The clear interprets the obscure.* Some passages in the Bible are very clear, others rather obscure. The principle of the clear interpreting the obscure means we won't interpret the obscure in such a way as to set it at variance with the clear. So, for example, whatever Paul meant by the obscure isolated reference to "the baptism for the dead" (1 Corinthians 15:29a), we will not read it to contradict the Bible's clear teaching on the decisiveness of our own decisions in this life in terms of our salvation and how these decisions affect life hereafter. Clearly, proxy baptism for the dead is not part of Paul's clear teaching about salvation. Perhaps then, while he's teaching about the Resurrection, he is referring to a practice of which he does not approve, nor one with which he identifies, only to point out that if people are mistakenly doing proxy baptisms for the dead, it clearly implies that they have a notion of Resurrection Life. Such could mean nothing "if the dead are not raised." (v. 29b) Whether that

is the right interpretation or not, my point is that we do not allow the obscure to confuse the clear. We interpret the obscure in the light of the clear.

7. *Scripture interprets Scripture.* This is almost a restatement of principle 6 above. We let different sections of Scripture shed light on others. For example, if we battle with the notion of a literal six-day period for Creation, maybe then we read the "days" of Genesis 1 in the light of the Bible's other word that "One day is with the Lord as a thousand years." (2 Peter 3:8) Maybe then we interpret Genesis 1 to mean God created in six great periods. So, too, if Paul says "We are justified by faith without the deeds of the law" (Romans 3:28), while James says "A man is justified by works and not by faith alone" (James 2:24), we don't set these Scriptures in contradiction, but see James correcting an abuse of faith which says we can trust Christ for our salvation and still live like the Devil. No! James is saying that if faith is alone without works, it is not real, saving faith at all! Paul agrees. Works are the fruit, though not the root, of saving faith and prove it. (See Ephesians 2:8-10) The person justified by faith must "apply himself to good works." (Titus 3:5-8) Indeed, says Paul, "it is not the hearers of the law who are righteous before God, but the doers of the law who will be justified." (Romans 2:13) So then, Ephesians 2:8-10 and Titus 3:5-8 interpret James 2:24 and vice versa. In other words, Scripture interprets Scripture. We approach one type of text through the lens of another.

Guidance

In addition to all the above principles, I believe we need also to believe God has given us three other teachers to instruct and guide us:

1. *The illumination of the Holy Spirit.* If the Spirit of God inspired the Bible and the biblical authors spoke from God, not on their own impulse, but as they were moved by the Holy Spirit (2 Peter 1:21), then it is the Holy Spirit who can best interpret what He

caused those original writers to write. This means that, for the humble, obedient believer, the Scriptures have, as noted earlier, what the Reformers called *claritas* (Latin for "clarity"). By this they meant the Scriptures had "understandability" through the illumination of the Holy Spirit. The Bible's basic meaning is not obscure. So the Reformers did not fear translating the Scriptures into the vernacular (English, French, German, etc.) so ordinary people who did not have a handle on Greek or medieval Latin could read them, understand them and obey them. The clerical authorities of the day much opposed this, thinking only they, with all their learning, could interpret the text. The Reformers rightly challenged this view.

2. *Our own reason*. We must exercise our God-given minds in a conscientious and humble way, not in order to stand in judgement on the Bible, but rather to submit to it, grapple with it, understand it and relate it to ourselves and the world around us.

3. *The teaching of the Church down the ages*. In the light of the two points above, we do not mean to say that the teaching of the Church is unimportant. To ignore what traditional Church theologians have said would be arrogant folly, although this does not mean that the Church and its theologians can never be wrong. So we do not accord to the Church or its tradition any infallible authority. We should reserve what the Reformers call "the right of private judgement", this being the birthright of every believer to hear the Father's voice coming to us directly through Scripture as interpreted and illuminated by the Holy Spirit.

Application

Then and only then comes the whole matter of application in our present historical context. This is the principle of cultural transposition. Having identified the essential revelation in the text, having made any necessary cultural separations from the cultural form in which it was originally given, we then re-clothe it in appropriate modern cultural terms and understandings. Our hermeneutic asks:

- What does the text say?
- What did the text mean then?
- What does the text mean for us now?
- How do I apply its meaning practically in my personal life and present context?

We can let the Spirit say to us, "Apply your whole self to the text. Apply the whole text to yourself."

Conclusion

In sum then, we see the Bible's own claim to be inspired or breathed out by God. We therefore accord it a very special species of final authority in our lives in all matters of faith and morals. We then apply sound principles of interpretation to the text so that we may not only understand what it says, what it means, and what it means for me, but then go out and obey it in the way we live in the world.

One person who did this unusually well was C.S. Lewis. So perhaps it is instructive to move from the theoretical to the personal and from thinking abstractly to being challenged concretely by one of the more extraordinary Christian thinkers of modern times.

Chapter Seven

Mere Christianity for Mere Christians

The Bible, in both Old and New Testaments, sees its central theme as the Messiah of God. For the New Testament, that means Jesus Christ. It is, therefore, salutary to pause and look at one life, namely that of C.S. Lewis, and see how he sought in honouring biblical authority, to face the claims of Jesus Christ and the Gospel in his own thought and life.

For the centennial year of the birth of C.S. Lewis in 1998 I interrupted my normal mission work in Africa to attend a two-week conference, called *Oxbridge '98*, held first in Oxford and then Cambridge. These were the universities where this great Christian layman spent the bulk of his working life. It was a great privilege to share and speak at this conference, whose significance for our present times is considerable – most particularly in its call to all Christians now to face the challenges of our present neo-pagan world culture with the same courage and resoluteness as Lewis did. We were privileged to meet his stepson, Douglas Gresham, who challenged the conference saying: "Jack (as C.S. Lewis liked to be called) did his part in his time. Now we must do it in ours."

"Loose in the fire"

For the 700 or so Church leaders, academics, authors and lay people from many places who listened to the opening address on this theme in the Oxford Church of St Mary the Virgin, it was a moving experience. For this was where the 16th century Archbishop of Canterbury, Thomas Cranmer, was tried in 1555 for his faith, convicted of heresy and sentenced to burn at the stake, a real case of being loose in the fire! Cranmer was the chief author and architect of the Anglican *Book of Common Prayer*, whose first edition came out in 1549. But Cranmer was too reformed, evangelical and Protestant to survive the heresy charges laid against him, even though he signed a number of recantations. He recanted through fear of suffering and through loyalty to the monarchy after being forced to watch the burning at the stake of fellow reformers Latimer and Ridley. However, he reversed these and on the eve of his execution, his courage returned. He went to the stake on March 21, 1556, denying his recantations and putting his right hand (which had signed the recantations) first into the fire, as a sign of repentance.

His fate followed that same "Loose in the fire" fate of Latimer and Ridley. Hugh Latimer, appointed Bishop of Worcester in 1535, was likewise a great reformer, expositor of the Scriptures, preacher and critic of the Church of his times. Doctrinally his emphasis was on justification by faith. He was very critical of his contemporaries in the Church, both clergy and bishops, and felt that under them biblical preaching had been betrayed and almost abandoned. In fact, "spurners of the truth" were getting away with it. This should not be! Sounds like C.S. Lewis!

Nicholas Ridley, consecrated Bishop of London in 1550, and another contributor to the 1552 revision of the Anglican *Book of Common Prayer*, was also an advocate of reformation and evangelical views, which led to his also going to the stake. As the fires were lit in Oxford (on a spot which, like a good tourist, I duly photographed while there), Latimer cried out to him, "Be of good comfort, Master Ridley, and play the man. We shall this day light such a candle by God's grace in England, as I trust shall never be put out."

So this was Oxford. This was the Church of St Mary the Virgin, Cranmer's place of trial. This was our heritage, both historically and theologically. This was also where Lewis preached on occasion, and this was July 1998 and the C.S. Lewis Centennial. No wonder we were impressed.

"Loose in the fire" was our conference theme, drawn not just from Oxford's history but also, more primarily, from Daniel 3.

There we are told Daniel's three friends, Shadrach, Meshach and Abednego, were thrown into the fire for not bowing down to Nebuchadnezzar, the golden image and the Babylonian gods (vv. 11-12). Then, to the astonishment of the king and his servants, the flames did not consume the three men, for in the furnace were seen, not three men loose in the fire, but four, "and the appearance of the fourth is like the Son of God" (v. 25, KJV). Jesus, in an Old Testament theophany, or visible manifestation of a deity, was present with those men. They refused to bow the knee to the false gods of their culture and time, even as Jesus will be now with all who stand against the spirit of the age and against our own false gods. Some of these are hedonism, philosophical materialism, naturalism, secularism, nationalism, tribalism, scepticism, immorality, promiscuity, ethical relativism, syncretism, "my-way-ism", ideological subjectivism (i.e. reality is finally determined by the individual), etc. To stand against these and against error, said *Oxbridge '98*, whether in culture, country or Church (and Lewis did all three) lands each of us loose in the fire.

The challenge before us

A friend of Lewis, Walter Hooper, described him as "the most thoroughly converted man I ever met."[44] Lewis made the challenge to take our conversion not only into every aspect of our daily lives, but into a creative and courageous challenge and interface with the world around us, which we are to seek not only to love but also to evangelise. "Woe to you if you do not evangelise,"[45] Lewis once warned some theological students!

Elsewhere he said, "Most of my books are evangelistic."[46] And the evangelistic issue with which we have to face our society and world is truth. Is an idea, a viewpoint, a doctrine, an ethic, "true or false", Lewis would ask, because for him, we do not commend or preach Christian faith just because it feels nice, is good or because it may help society, "but because it is true." And the fundamental issue relates to the truth or otherwise of the incarnation of God in Jesus Christ. Is that true or false? Did it or did it not happen?

Are we the "invaded planet" by God Himself, or are we not? Is this true or false? Of course, our Postmodernist culture, which only allows us opinion statements and not truth statements, squirms at such a challenge. We will still discuss this further.

The challenge from Lewis is that we must insist that Christianity and Jesus are either all-important or not important at all. Thus could he write: "One must keep pointing out that Christianity is a statement which, if false is of *no* importance, and, if true, of *infinite* importance. The one thing it cannot be is moderately important."[47] So, first of all, we must decide, then we must help our world decide. What about the claims of Christ? Are they true or false? All this brings us to the heart of the matter – that is, to Jesus and His claims.

Jesus as the heart of the matter

On Jesus' claims, made in the context of monotheistic, Old Testament Judaism, Lewis writes in his inimitable style as follows, giving us a thorough feel for his central message: "Then comes the real shock. Among these Jews there suddenly turns up a man who goes about talking as if He was God. He claims to forgive sins. He says He has always existed. He says He is coming to judge the world at the end of time.

"Now let us get this clear. Among pantheists, like the Indians, anyone might say that he was a part of God, or one with God, there would be nothing very odd about it. But this man, since He was a Jew, could not mean that kind of God. God, in their language, meant the being outside the world, who had made it and was infinitely different from anything else. And when you have grasped that, you will see that what this man said was, quite simply, the most shocking thing that has ever been uttered by human lips. One part of the claim tends to slip past us unnoticed because we have heard it so often that we no longer see what it amounts to. I mean the claim to forgive sins, any sins. Now, unless the speaker is God, this is really so preposterous as to be comic. We can all understand how a man forgives offences against himself. You tread on my toe and I forgive you, you steal my money and I forgive you. But what should we make of a man, himself unrobbed and untrodden on, who announced that he forgave you for treading on other people's toes and stealing other people's money? Asinine fatuity is the kindest description we should give of his conduct. Yet this is what Jesus did. He told people that their sins were forgiven, and never waited to consult all the other people whom their sins had undoubtedly injured. He unhesitatingly behaved as if He was the party chiefly concerned, the person chiefly offended in all offences. This makes sense only if He really was the God whose laws are broken and whose love is wounded in every sin. In the mouth of any speaker who is not God, these words would imply what I can only regard as a silliness and conceit unrivalled by any other character in history. Yet (and this is the strange, significant thing) even His enemies, when they read the Gospels, do not usually get the impression of silliness and conceit. Still less do unprejudiced readers. Christ says that He is 'humble and meek' and we believe Him; not noticing that, if He were merely a man, humility and meekness are the very last characteristics we could attribute to some of His sayings. I am trying here to prevent anyone saying the really foolish thing that people often say about Him, 'I am ready to accept Jesus as a great moral teacher, but I do not accept His claim to be God.' That is the one thing we must not say. A man who was merely a man and said the sort of things Jesus said would not be a great moral teacher. He would either be a lunatic – on a level with the man who says he is a poached egg – or else he would be the Devil of Hell. You must make your choice. Either this man was, and is, the Son of God, or else a madman or something worse. You can shut Him up for a fool, you can spit at Him and kill Him as a demon; or you can fall at His feet and call Him Lord and God. But let us not come with any patronising nonsense about His being a great human teacher. He has not left that open to us. He did not intend to.[48]

Face-to-face with a verdict

All of this, says Lewis, means each of us is faced with a decision to reach a verdict about Jesus: it is not just an intellectual decision; it has to be volitional. It is not just mind but also will, not just what we will believe about Him, but whether we will trust, follow and surrender to Him. There has to be a giving up of ourselves, but this is not so bad, because when we do so, we not only find life, we find ourselves. A startling discovery that can be somewhat shocking at times, but a very important one.

Listen again to Lewis, from the very end of his book *Mere Christianity*: "The more we get what we now call 'ourselves' out of the way and let him take us over, the more truly ourselves we become. There is so much of him that millions and millions of 'little Christs', all different, will still be too few to express him fully. He made them all. He invented – as an author invents characters in a novel – all the different men and women that you and I were intended to be. In that sense, our real selves are all waiting for us in Him. It is no good trying to 'be myself' without Him. The more I resist Him and try to live on my own, the more I become dominated by my own heredity and upbringing and surroundings and natural desires. In fact, what I so proudly call 'myself' becomes merely the meeting place for trains of events which I never started and which I cannot stop. What I call 'my wishes' become merely the desires thrown up by my physical organism or pumped into me by other men's thoughts or even suggested to me by devils. Propaganda will be the real origin of what I regard as my own personal political ideals. I am not, in my natural state, nearly so much of a person as I like to believe; most of what I call 'me' can be very easily explained. It is when I turn to Christ, when I give myself up to His personality, that I first begin to have a real personality of my own."[49]

Lewis brings us to the crunch, the giving of ourselves to Christ. We might call it the challenge of self-surrender.

The challenge of self-surrender

Again from the end of *Mere Christianity*, Lewis confronts us with the great volitional leap of faith. This is not a leap in the dark but rather a leap based on reason, truth, history and a sufficiency of evidences. We can, he says, find ourselves as we find God in self-surrender. "But there must be a real giving up of the self. You must throw it away 'blindly' so to speak. Christ will indeed give you a real personality, but you must not go to Him for the sake of that.

As long as your own personality is what you are bothering about you are not going to him at all. The very first step is to try to forget about the self altogether. Your real, new self (which is Christ's and also yours, and yours just because it is His), will not come as long as you are looking for it. It will come when you are looking for Him. Does that sound strange? "The same principle holds, you know, for more everyday matters. Even in social life, you will never make a good impression on other people until you stop thinking about what sort of impression you are making. Even in literature and art, no person who bothers about originality will ever be original, whereas if you simply try to tell the truth (without caring twopence how often it has been told before) you will, nine times out of ten, become original without ever having noticed it. The principle runs through all life from top to bottom. Give up yourself, and you will find your real self. Lose your life and you will save it. Submit to death, death of your ambitions and favourite wishes every day and death of your whole body in the end, submit with every fibre of your being, and you will find eternal life. Keep back nothing. Nothing that you have not given away will ever be really yours. Nothing in you that has not died will ever be raised from the dead. Look for yourself, and you will find in the long run only hatred, loneliness, despair, rage, ruin, and decay. But look for Christ and you will find Him, and with Him everything else thrown in."[50]

This is true and this is the heart of the faith. Mere Christianity, you might say, and for mere Christians like you and me.

Conclusion

In this chapter we have only touched C.S. Lewis' thought and the challenges of *Oxbridge '98*. But I hope it has whetted your appetite to explore him further.[51]

I close this chapter with one of Lewis' celebrated quotes, relevant to all who face both the lostness of our culture and the confusion often prevalent in the contemporary Church: "Paul told us to be not only as harmless as doves but as wise as serpents. And Christ wants (from us) a child's heart, but a grown up's head."[52]

This is particularly true as we look further at Jesus Christ. We use our heads to face His claims and decide who He is. Then, grasping that He is none other than God in the flesh, the Lord of the universe and of history, our Saviour and Redeemer, we come to Him like little children and in childlike faith present ourselves to Him.

8

Chapter Eight

The Uniqueness, Resurrection and Deity of Jesus Christ

C.S. Lewis, who honoured the Bible and the Christ portrayed there, has launched us on the first part of really getting to grips with the Person of Jesus as the central figure and theme of the Bible. In fact, if we are truly eager to be "getting to the heart of things" then getting to Jesus, as the Scriptures portray Him, is a high-priority item.

Let's pursue this further.

Jesus is of course the central Person of the Christian faith. I believe that He is indeed the central figure in all of history and even now, the world's fascination with Him remains. In recent years, both *Time* and *Newsweek* magazines have had cover stories on Jesus and the Gospels. Philip Yancey, in *The Jesus I Never Knew*, speaks of Him as "the great divide of human history" and asserts, "No one who meets Jesus ever stays the same."[53] True, amazingly true. That is why I want to explore Jesus' uniqueness, that is, the ways in which He is unlike any other human being or religious leader who ever lived.

Uniqueness in mystery

First of all, Jesus was unique in mystery. To be face to face with Him is to face mystery. An anonymous writer once wrote, "Nineteen centuries have come and gone and today He is the central figure of the human race. All the armies that ever marched, all the navies that ever sailed, all the parliaments that ever sat, all the kings that ever reigned, put together, have not affected the life of people on this earth as much as that one solitary life." There is mystery in that influence and impact, as well as in Jesus' ongoing capacity, even in a materialistic age such as ours, to draw people to Himself.

Uniqueness of prophetic fulfilment

Being Jews, the first followers of Jesus had the highest regard for the Old Testament, which enshrined the oracles of God. Yet it can be seen to be manifestly incomplete because it spoke of a day when God would judge the earth. It spoke of a king of David's stock whose dominion would be boundless. It spoke of all the families of humankind – not just Jewish ones – being blessed in Abraham. It spoke of a messianic Son of Man inaugurating a kingdom that would never be destroyed. Indeed, in scores of places in the Old Testament, there are prophecies pointing to a Messiah and to various aspects of His life and work. We firstly see Bethlehem as His prophesied birthplace (Micah 5:2), and finally Isaiah tells us of the One who will bear our iniquities (Isaiah 53:6-7). He will be the "Lamb of God" sacrificing Himself for our sins. No one fits all this but Jesus. In fact, there are some 300 Old Testament prophecies about the Messiah to come and Christians believe that these are indeed manifestly fulfilled in Jesus Christ. It has been calculated "that for Jesus to have fulfilled these 300-odd prophecies purely by chance could be expressed mathematically as one chance in 10^{181}, or one chance in 10 plus 180 more zeros. A fair mind will agree this did not happen by chance."[54] And to be sure, Jesus saw Himself as the fulfilment of all the Old Testament messianic prophecies.

Luke the historian reports, "And beginning with Moses and all the prophets, He [Jesus] interpreted to them in all the Scriptures the things concerning Himself" (Luke 24:27). Extraordinary!

Uniqueness in His birth

There was also amazing uniqueness in the birth of Jesus. The Gospels are clear that, though Joseph was the legal father of Jesus, he was not His biological father. We are told that Jesus was born by the direct action of the Holy Spirit of God, the source of all life, in the womb of Mary, His mother, who was at that time still a virgin. Certainly Joseph was startled enough about his fiancée's pregnancy and "resolved to divorce her quietly" (Matthew 1:19). He knew *he* was not the father.

Unique in the things He said and the claims He made

People were staggered by Jesus' utterances long before His peerless character astounded them. Enemies sent to trap Him said, "No man ever spoke like this man!" (John 7:46) Furthermore, "the crowds were astonished at His teaching, for He taught them as one who had authority, and not as their scribes" (Matthew 7:28-29). But we must also note in Jesus something without precedent in the span of human literature. While urging humility on others and while giving the impression of being the ultimate humble person, Jesus' teaching and claims are egocentric and completely focussed on Himself. In ordinary life, that would label a person as crazy or as a megalomaniac! Just think of a few astounding claims Jesus made about Himself: "I am the resurrection and the life" (John 11:25); "I am the bread of life" (John 6:35); "I am the light of the world" (John 8:12, 9:5); "I am the good shepherd" (John 10:11, 14); "I am the door … " (John 10:7,9); " … whoever lives and believes in Me shall never die" (John 11:26); and "He who has seen Me has seen the Father" (John 14:9).

In no other religion does one find any even remotely comparable claims. Moreover, the fact that Jesus cannot be ranked among a pantheon of religious leaders or options becomes obvious when one reflects further on His claim of being at both the beginning and the end of creation and of history. He said, "I am the first and the last" (Revelation 1:17), as well as, "All authority in heaven and on earth has been given to me" (Matthew 28:18). Clearly the disciples accepted this, as John begins his Gospel with these words: "In the beginning was the Word, and the Word was with God, *and the Word was God* … all things were made through Him, and without Him was not anything made that was made ... And the Word became flesh and made His dwelling among us" (John 1:1,3,14; italics mine). Says Paul: "for in Him all things were created ... and in Him all things hold together" (Colossians 1:16,17).

When we look at what Jesus says about the end of history, we are even more startled, as when He said of any person who follows Him, "I will raise him up at the last day" (John 6:40). Remember, this was the local carpenter! And when we note that throughout the Bible final judgement is a function reserved to God alone, it is astounding to register that Jesus says of Himself, "For as the Father has life in Himself, so He has granted the Son also to have life in Himself, and has given Him authority to execute judgement, because He is the Son of Man" (John 5:26-27). Yes, between creation and the end of history stands Jesus. That also means, of course, and we note it with comfort, that everything in between is His also. There is no claim like it anywhere. It stands alone, unique.

Unique in His deeds, actions and character

As extraordinary as Jesus' claims were, they were (not surprisingly) backed up by remarkable and often supernatural actions. When Jesus cured a paralytic, Mark says, "This amazed everyone and they praised God, saying, 'We never saw anything like this!'" (Mark 2:12) Not only did Jesus heal sick and disabled people, He raised to life people who had died. When He brought Lazarus back to life, John says, "Many of the Jews therefore, who had come with Mary and had seen what He did, believed in Him" (John 11:45). Furthermore, Jesus demonstrated power over nature and the elements, such as when He calmed the storm and commanded the wind and the sea to be peaceful (Mark 4:35-41). Here also was an entire life that was a consistent, faultless and unsurpassed catalogue of incredible love and care for the afflicted, the bereaved, the downcast, the widow, the outcast and the lonely.

Deeds and actions flow out from who a person actually is, so it is not surprising to find that Jesus' character was unassailable. Indeed, all lives are measured by His, and His life is measured by no one else's. In this vein, we must note His challenge: "Which of you convicts Me of sin?" (John 8:46) Certainly, our planet can bestow no higher accolade on a person than to say he or she is "Christlike". This is because there was no gap between what Jesus taught and who He was. Intimate friends said He was "a lamb without blemish or spot" (1 Peter 1:19), one who "committed no sin" and in whose mouth was found "no guile" (1 Peter 2:22). John the Apostle, one of His very closest associates, affirmed, "and in Him there is no sin." (1 John 3:5). Even His enemies conceded this point. A Roman centurion asked, "What evil has He done?" (Matthew 27:23) And Judas Iscariot lamented, "I have sinned in betraying innocent blood" (Matthew 27:4).

Uniqueness in the climactic events related to the end of Jesus' earthly life

Other people throughout history have been executed, some by crucifixion, the most cruel form of capital punishment ever devised by humankind. But no one other than Jesus had predicted His sacrificial death by saying: "For the Son of man also came not to be served but to serve, and to give His life as a ransom for many" (Mark 10:45). Furthermore, no one had allowed his or her death to be linked to the whole Jewish Old Testament sacrificial system, as when Jesus accepted the words of John the Baptist: "Behold, the Lamb of God, who takes away the sin of the world!" (John 1:29)

However, as unique as Jesus' death was, it could not compare with the awesome event three days later, of His resurrection. In many ways, though, given all we have said about Jesus, it would have been more surprising if He had not risen from the dead! Even so, many people have trouble coming to terms with Jesus' resurrection and are inclined to doubt it. But if we really look closely at the evidence for and against, as well as other possible explanations, we will surely come to a conclusion similar to that of Sir Edward Clarke, a distinguished English attorney, who wrote, "As a lawyer I have made a prolonged study of the evidences for the events of the first Easter day. To me the evidence is conclusive, and over and over again in the High Court I have secured the verdict on evidence not nearly so compelling."[55]

When the Bible says that Jesus presented Himself alive on that Sunday morning to the women at the tomb and later to many others, some object that it must have been some sort of trick. But we know from Jesus' unimpeachable character that He would never have been party to such deceit. Nor could He have been some sort of a ghost or apparition because ghosts, as He said, do not have "flesh and bones as you see that I have" (Luke 24:39). Nor could people have been seeing hallucinations since hallucinations cannot be physically handled. They also tend to come to individuals and not to clusters of people, such as the 12 disciples – or to 500 people at one time! Nor would they happen frequently for six weeks and then suddenly cease. Again, the resurrection could not have been the result of some sort of wish-fulfilment, because the disciples were not expecting Jesus to live again. Indeed, they dismissed the first reports of the resurrection from the women because their words "seemed to them an idle tale" (Luke 24:11).

Also, we are not dealing with a fabrication, for what did the disciples stand to gain, aside from ostracism and martyrdom? And why would anyone want to suffer so for a lie? They might bear persecution for some self-deception or illusion, but not for something they know to be fraudulent.

Nor could this have been a deception of the disciples based on a stolen body, for Roman guards were stationed at the tomb to prevent such a thing happening. And who could have stolen the body? Friends or disciples could not have got past the guards even if they had had the courage, a quality they conspicuously lacked. Indeed, the Bible says they all fled after Jesus was crucified and we know Peter would not even admit to being a follower of Jesus the night of His arrest.

If foes had stolen the body, why did they not produce it when the disciples began preaching the resurrection? That would have collapsed the resurrection claims like a house of cards! They did not produce the body because they could not. Finally, it could not have been a case of the disciples going to a mistaken tomb. After all, Jesus had been buried in a private tomb donated by a sympathetic wealthy man. It was not, for example, as if He was buried in one of 100,000 or so indistinguishable graves of a New York cemetery.

Witnesses

No, Jesus had risen from the dead for sure – for "historical sure" – and could and did subsequently present Himself alive to many people. Certainly for multitudes down the ages, the evidence for the resurrection is overwhelming and compelling and we can agree with Lord Darling, a former Chief Justice of England, who said, "The crux of the problem of whether Jesus was, or was not, what He proclaimed Himself to be, must surely depend upon the truth or otherwise of the resurrection. On that greatest point we are not merely asked to have faith. In its favour as a living truth there exists such overwhelming evidence, positive and negative, factual and circumstantial, that no intelligent jury in the world could fail to bring in a verdict that the resurrection story is true."[56]

Uniqueness of Christian experience

Any of us who have come to see Jesus as unique and as the Son of God, who died sacrificially to atone for our sins and then rose again in divine glory, know that from the time we surrendered our lives to Him, we also had it experientially confirmed that He is who He said He was and that the Bible is true in its description and accounts of Him. We know it from our personal experience of Him as Saviour, Master, Lord and Friend and from the change He has brought into our lives. Said Paul, " … if anyone is in Christ, he is a new creation; the old has passed away, behold, the new has come" (2 Corinthians 5:17).

Augustine said, "Thou didst put gladness in my heart." In evangelistic work, one hears every week of people who have had their lives transformed by Christ, often radically. The old hymn captures this experience well: "You ask me how I know He lives/He lives within my heart." Twenty centuries of believers can affirm that.

Uniqueness in His survival of massive intellectual assaults

Even in the Church today – and indeed through the last two centuries or so – some would not endorse our conviction of the deity of Christ. And even in theological colleges, some become part of a unique measure of assault on Jesus. Others are patronisingly kind and include Him as one among many in a pantheon of great religious and spiritual leaders, including Buddha, Confucius, Muhammad and even Abraham and Moses. Many in our modern and increasingly Postmodern era even view the notion of a divine Jesus as antiquated, unenlightened, nonessential or part of a narrow intolerance of other religious beliefs. I believe these views can only be sustained if one plays havoc with the Scriptures, and approaches them with naturalistic presuppositions that deny anything supernatural. This rejection by presupposition is tragic, like a child saying there is no such thing as 13 x 13, just because they have only gone to 12 x 12 in arithmetic!

Sadly, rejecting Jesus' supernaturalness on the basis of presupposition is not new. Says German theologian Helmut Thielicke in *How Modern Should Theology Be?*: "Again and again the package of divine truth has been opened and everything which did not suit was laid aside. Over and over, the figure of Jesus has been horribly amputated until He fit ... what one particular age held to be 'modern' concepts ... Through the whole history of the Church Jesus Christ has suffered a process of repeated crucifixion. He has been scourged and bruised and locked in the prison of countless systems and philosophies. Treated as a body of thought, He has literally been lowered into conceptual graves and covered with stone slabs so that He might not arise and trouble us any more. Has not this process rendered Him harmless by enrolling Him in the club of human thought? ... Is not the history of the Church to the present day one vast experiment gone awry, a dreadful victory of the currently 'modern' over the Nazarene who must bear it all helplessly and silently?"[57]

But, asserts Thielicke, "No mere thought, you see, could ever have survived such strong medicine. No human idea could have endured such attacks, amputations, and crucifixions without ending in the graveyard of intellectual history, where only the historian would still find anything worthwhile. But this is the miracle, that from this succession of conceptual graves Jesus Christ has risen again and again! None of them became His last resting place. No tombstone was ever heavy enough to hold Him. Again and again, wherever two or three are gathered in His name, He steps into their midst and is present with His strength and consolation. Again and again He appears at the deathbed and holds up the head of the sufferer in his final weakness. And people face death for Him with songs of praise on their lips. By the now-empty grave, however, the angel asks us also, 'Why do you seek the living among the dead? Your graves too could not hold Him.' The fact that we gather in congregations, that we hear His word, speak with Him and praise Him – this is the great refutation of that tragic vision which sees people burying the living Lord in their conceptual graves and making Him a harmless 'historical figure.'"[58]

Thielicke sums up with a bold and encouraging statement: "Be comforted and unafraid, for I say to you now in His name, Jesus Christ Himself is already far out in front of every age that attempts to come to grips with Him. He sees to that. He is more up-to-date than any 'modern' age that feels itself superior to all that has gone before. His promise still holds true for us. He is always the newest and most up-to-the-minute on this old-fashioned earth, the Living One on the field of dead bones. For He said, 'Behold I am with you always, even unto the end of the world.'"[59]

That is gloriously true, even in these pluralistic times. And this being so, we can hardly hold back from preaching Jesus unashamedly to one and all, whoever and wherever they are, as "the Saviour of the world" (John 4:42). For "there is salvation in no one else, for there is no other name under heaven given among men by which we must be saved" (Acts 4:12).

And, of course, as we preach Him, our major focus has to be the Cross. As the Apostle Paul said to the Corinthians: "I decided to know nothing among you except Jesus Christ and Him crucified" (1 Corinthians 2:2).

And so that glorious, central theme we now turn more fully.

Chapter Nine

The Cross as the Real Heart of Things

Strangely enough my own commitment to Christ happened without any clear understanding of the Cross of Christ or the atonement. I was able somehow or other to turn to Christ and be converted to Him, without grasping much of the meaning and place of the Cross. But in the normal run of things people do come to some understanding of the Cross before they are able to turn their lives over to the One who died on the Cross.

However, fairly soon into my Christian life I did begin to grasp something of what it was all about and could echo the words of a devoted soul who once wrote:

> *A crossless Christ my Saviour could not be*
> *A Christless cross no refuge is for me*
> *But oh, Christ crucified, I rest on Thee.*

Christians believe we will never understand the Cross until we grasp something of the nature and awfulness of human sin and rebellion which the Cross ultimately addresses.

Sin defined

The New Testament has different words for sin, each of which brings a distinctive meaning.

The first of these is *hamartia*. This Greek word basically means missing the mark or a failure to hit the target. In the Christian scriptures it basically means falling short of God's standards and missing the mark of His perfect requirements of us. It is a word predominantly used for wrong action and always carries the idea of going astray. Thus the apostle can write in Romans 3:23: "For all have sinned and come short of the glory of God."

The second significant word for sin is *paraptoma*. This speaks of a slip or fall or someone straying from the right road and getting lost. It speaks of humans failing to grasp truth adequately and then slipping away from it. The verb form *parapipto* (e.g. in Hebrews 6:6) means "to commit a fault." Thus in Matthew 6:14 it is a fault against others and in verse 15 a fault against God. In normal parlance, we think of a slip as something pretty minor, as with "a slip of the tongue" or "he had a little moral slip", or we might describe someone saying that "she slipped away from the truth." But as with a car slipping on a muddy road, the consequences can be drastic.

Thirdly, there is the word *parabasis*. This means overstepping the mark, getting into transgression or violating the law. The issue here is not by how much we overstep the mark or how significantly we transgress, but simply the fact that we do. If I drive at 102 kilometres per hour within a 100-kilometre speed zone, I have nevertheless overstepped the mark and am in violation of the law. I am guilty. And spiritually, in New Testament terms, when I overstep the mark, even in a minor way, I commit sin. In fact, in the New Testament, this word specifically denotes sin in relation to the law. So, for example, in Romans 2:23 the apostle says that the Jew dishonours God by transgressing the law and in Romans 4:15 the apostle says that law brings God's wrath on us because there is transgression (*parabasis*) only where there is law. Says Kittel's famous Wordbook: "Between Adam and Moses there is sin but no *parabasis* because the law is not yet given. In Galatians 3:19 the law is given to show that evil deeds are transgressions of God's will."[60] Anytime we "step over the line", another of the meanings of this word, we are sinning and in need of the atoning forgiveness of Christ.

There are a couple of other words we should not miss out on at this point. One is *adikia* which means unrighteousness or iniquity. Then there is an even stronger word, *poneria*, which speaks of evil of a very vicious or degenerate nature. The notion is of inward corruption or even perversion of character.

The last word to note is *anomia*. This means lawlessness or kicking over the traces. The Greek word at the root of *anomia* is *nomos*, meaning law, and it normally denotes the Pentateuch, though in the New Testament it can refer to the Old Testament as a whole. *Nomos* speaks primarily about that which governs conduct and behaviour. Breaking the law in the Old Testament could in certain instances mean the death penalty. The point is that if the law is indeed the good will of God, then to oppose it is to oppose God. (See Romans 8:7). Thus it is that the Lord demands right action. Obeying the law is something one does. (Romans 2:25). It represents God's living will and as such it speaks about what He requires us to do. But because of our human sinfulness we cannot achieve everything the law requires us to do. This tells us that we are sinners who need a Saviour.

If all of that is true, and if we are sinners to this degree, then how can we escape or avoid judgement if we are the creation of a fully righteous and completely just God?

Law brings the knowledge of sin

It is obviously then also true that as we see the almost impossibly exalted and high standards of God in the law that we come to realise that we cannot achieve those standards and therefore see that we are sinners and guilty before the law. Says the Apostle Paul in Romans 3:19: "Now we know that whatever the law says, it speaks to those that are under the law, so that every mouth may be stopped, and the whole world may be held accountable to God. For no human being will be justified in His sight by works of the law, since through the law comes the knowledge of sin." In other words, seeing what the law requires tells us we are sinners.

So the apostle can write likewise in Galatians 3:24: "So the law was our schoolmaster to bring us to Christ so that we might be justified by faith." Says Paul: "If it had not been for the law, I should have not have known sin" (Romans 7:7).

What all this does is put a choice before the human race. We can either seek to operate outside of faith in Christ, in which case we put ourselves under the law (Colossians 2:20) and are obliged to keep it fully down to every detail. If we can't or don't do this, we put ourselves under judgement. But if we choose rather to come to the Cross of Christ and to the grace and mercy of God, then we are no longer under the law but experience a translation from the sphere of law into the sphere of grace and sonship. In Christ we are freed from the demands of the law as a way of salvation, even if we could fulfil the law's requirements. That's why those who still seek righteousness through the law are declaring Christ's death to be in vain. Writes the apostle: "So I do not nullify the grace of God; for if justification were through the law, then Christ died to no purpose" (Galatians 2:21).

In fact, if we try to hang in with the demands of the law and fulfilling the works of the law, then we put ourselves under what the apostle calls "a curse." Says he: "For all who rely on works of the law are under a curse; for it is written 'cursed be everyone who does not abide *by all things written in the book of the law and do them ... '"* ... "But Christ has redeemed us from the curse of the law, having become a curse for us – for it is written, 'cursed be everyone who hangs on a tree'" (Galatians 3;10, 13).

So there is an antithesis between the way of the law and trying to fulfil its requirements, and the way of faith which enables us to reach out and receive salvation as the free gift of God made available on the basis of His mercy alone and through Christ's atoning death on the cross. Therefore, says the apostle: "We hold that a person is justified by faith apart from the works of the law" (Romans 3:28).

So then, coming back to our last key word, *anomia*, we register that the prefix "a", meaning "away from" or "without", conveys the sense of a total absence of law or a total non-observance of it. In other words, lawlessness. It speaks about those who have no law or who pay no attention to law. These are people who have gone morally and spiritually AWOL. And of course on top of all that are sins of omission when we do not do the things we should, and when we have left undone those things we ought to have done.

Judgement, punishment and forgiveness

Given what we have said above, we realise as creatures of this living God that we are in a serious moral predicament and absolutely lost, unforgivable and unredeemable. And we can do nothing about it. That is, unless God Himself should do something about it. To be sure He cannot overlook our sin and stay true to His holiness. So what is to happen?

This leads us into the realms of punishment and forgiveness and the various options which can operate.

1. *Punishment and no forgiveness.* This is the realm of the army, the military or the law court. For example, when a soldier betrays his mates or disobeys his commanding officer there is military punishment meted out and with no forgiveness. Or in the legal arena, the accused is brought before the judge for having murdered someone. The judge pronounces a life sentence and decrees the punishment and there is no forgiveness.

2. *Forgiveness and no punishment.* This is the realm of human relationships. A man commits adultery and his wife forgives him but does not punish him. A colleague at work bad-mouths you, and you forgive him without punishing him.

3. *Forgiveness and punishment, but the punishment is borne by the offending person.* This is the realm, for example, of the schoolmaster. A schoolboy does something naughty and the teacher punishes the youngster by gaiting him or as in past times, giving him a hiding! The schoolmaster then restores the boy to favour and fellowship. Both forgiveness and punishment are there but the punishment is borne by the offending person.

4. *Forgiveness and punishment, but the punishment is borne by the one offended.* This is the realm of the God and Father of our Lord Jesus Christ who manifests perfect justice in decreeing the

penalty and then in perfect love paying it Himself. This is the arena where punishment is borne by the offended in order to forgive the offender. Thus it is that law says "you sin, you pay." But God's grace says "you sin, I pay." This is where the Cross becomes the cost to God of His act of forgiveness to wayward humans. So it is that when we ask, "How far will God go with us?", the Cross answers, *"All the way!"*

Atonement

Before we get into some metaphors of atonement, let's reflect a moment on the word itself.

The atonement, for all who take biblical truth seriously is the centre of gravity both for Christian life and thought and for the entire message of the New Testament. The atonement also exposes for us the divine dilemma as to how God could be holy and true to His holiness and justice and at the same time justify or forgive His disobedient human creations. The question is how a holy God could love and accept sinners without compromising His own character, destroying His holiness, or sentimentalising His love into a weak and immoral indifference to sin and wrong. In other words, how can God bring wayward humans into "at-one-ment" with Himself?

Of course trying to fathom the full meaning of the cross will always leave us at a place of mystery, perplexity and enigma. The fact is that in many ways Calvary is an unfathomable mystery for human minds.

However, what we do know is that as we look at these metaphors our hearts have to begin to sing:

> *Bearing shame and scoffing rude,*
> *In my place condemned He stood;*
> *Sealed my pardon with His blood:*
> *Hallelujah! What a Saviour!*

Metaphors of atonement

Now to these four very instructive metaphors of atonement:

Jesus as Lamb of God
In John 1:29 we read of John the Baptist hailing Jesus with these words: "Behold the Lamb of God who takes away the sin of the world." At that moment John the Baptist was invoking the whole Old Testament sacrificial system and connecting that system and its meanings to the death which Jesus would one day die as "a Lamb without spot and blemish" (1 Peter 1:19) bearing the sin of the whole world. Thus, early in Jesus' life and public ministry a strong identification is made between His death and the prophetic fulfilment of the Old Testament Passover. Writes the Apostle Paul: "Christ, our Passover Lamb has been sacrificed. Therefore let us keep the festival ... " (1 Corinthians 5:7-8).

The story of course takes us back to the climactic moments prior to the Exodus of the Israelites out of Egypt, as recorded in Exodus 12 and 13. Each household of the Israelite nation was to take a lamb without blemish (v. 5), slay it (v. 6) and then take some of that blood and put it on the doorposts and on the lintel of the Israelite houses (v. 7). They were about to participate in "the Lord's Passover" (v. 11). It was to be a night of judgement and death for the firstborn, both man and beast, of the Egyptians. God would smite them and execute His judgements upon them (v. 12). Then the Lord speaks and says: "The blood shall be a sign for you, upon the houses where you are; and when I see the blood, I will pass over, and no plague shall fall upon you to destroy you, when I smite the land of Egypt. This day shall be for you a memorial day, and you shall keep it as a feast to the Lord; throughout your generations you shall observe it as an ordinance forever" (Exodus 12:13-14).

Here we see our Lord God beginning to teach us how He could express simultaneously both His holiness in judgement and then His love in pardon. The only way would be by providing a God-given substitute for the sinner, so that the substitute would bear the judgement and the sinner receive the pardon.

In New Testament perspective then Jesus, the Lamb of God,

becomes the substitute for the sinner so that the sinner may be spared.

Of course the whole import of the book of Hebrews is that the blood sacrifices of the Old Testament were only shadows and pictures of the true substance to come which was Jesus and His sacrificial death on the cross for us. No wonder Peter could speak of "the precious blood of Christ" which had been shed for him and for us all. (1 Peter 1:19).

Another vivid image comes from Isaiah 53:6 where the prophet writes that "all we like sheep have gone astray; we have turned everyone to his own way, and the Lord has laid on the Suffering Servant the iniquity of us all."

Stressing that the essence of the atonement is the substitutionary death of Christ, John Stott notes both eloquently and succinctly that: "The concept of substitution may be said ... to lie at the heart of both sin and salvation. For the essence of sin is man substituting himself for God, while the essence of salvation is God substituting Himself for man. Man asserts himself against God and puts himself where only God deserves to be; God sacrifices Himself for man and puts Himself where only man deserves to be. Man claims prerogatives which belong to God alone; God accepts penalties which belong to man alone."[61]

Jesus as Penalty-Bearer
If the first image of Jesus as Lamb of God was taken from the Old Testament sacrificial system, the second image of Jesus as penalty-bearer is taken from the realm of the law courts. Says the Apostle Peter: "He Himself bore our sins in His own body on the tree" (1 Peter 2:26).

To understand this better one might take the illustration of being pulled over in your car for speeding by a traffic cop who turns out to be a good friend of yours. You are fond of each other and have a fine friendship. But the hard legal fact is that you have broken the law and you properly deserve to be punished. But the person who has caught you is a friend who loves you. The dilemma for the traffic cop is how to be true to his justice, as representing the law at that moment, and also true to his loving attitude to you which makes him want to free you, forgive you and release you. The dilemma for him is acute. If he simply releases you and forgives you out of his love, he is a bad traffic cop because he is trivialising his role as a representative of the law and as one who personalises justice at that moment. But if only his justice operates, then he is sad out of his love for you to see you suffer the penalty. What is he to do? The answer is for him in his justice to decree the penalty and in his love to pay it himself. Thus it is that he writes out the charge slip which condemns you and informs you that a fine of R500 is to be paid. He has been true to his justice. But then his loving and forgiving spirit kicks in and he takes out his own chequebook and writes a cheque payable to the Magistrate's Court for R500. In his justice he has condemned you for your crime but in his love he has paid the penalty for you himself.

And that is exactly what God has done. In His holiness and justice He has decreed the penalty of death and declared from Genesis to Revelation that "the wages of sin is death" (Romans 6:23). The penalty God's justice requires has been properly and appropriately decreed. But then in His great love and compassion, God in Christ has come to Planet Earth to bear in His love the spiritual death penalty which He had previously decreed in His justice. At the Cross both the justice and the love of God meet and find resolution with each other.

Glory to God, the divine pardon can now reach me.

Jesus as Ransom-Payer
This is a similar image to the one above, but more related to the law courts. Paul writes in Galatians 4:4-7: "When the time had fully come God sent forth His Son ... to redeem those who were under the law so that we might receive adoption as sons. And because you are sons, God has sent the Spirit of the Son into our hearts, crying, 'Abba! Father!' So through God you are no longer a slave but a son, and if a son then an heir." The two key notions here are *redemption* (which means paying the price to purchase a slave) and *adoption* (which means bringing into one's family, who is not by nature and birth one's child, but who becomes such by the adopting process).

Now here's my next little illustration, bearing in mind that in both Old and New Testaments God is referred to as a judge. Thus the words of Genesis 18:25: "Shall not the judge of all the earth do right?" In the New Testament the apostle says: "We will all appear before the judgement seat of Christ" (2 Corinthians 5:10). So now, visualise a little orphan boy who loves breaking glass, whether windows, vases, water glasses or whatever. Finally the little orphan boy is brought before the judge of the town to be faced with his crimes of vandalism. The judge sees the seriousness of the crime and in his justice cannot overlook it or he would be a bad judge. But his heart of loving compassion goes out to the little boy. So what is he to do? First of all he decrees the penalty of R1000 and then, as with the traffic cop, he takes out his chequebook and writes a cheque for R1000 to the court. In his justice he condemned the little boy, decreed the penalty, and then in his love paid the penalty himself. But his heart of love goes even further. Recognising that the little boy is an orphan, he decides to adopt him into his own family. So, first of all there was a ransom or a redemption paid to secure the little boy's release from the consequences of his crime. He does not now have to pay the penalty himself. Then secondly there is an adopting act whereby the little boy is now brought into the family of the judge. The judge now becomes his father.

We then have to ask whether the little boy's nature changes overnight. And of course the answer is that it does not. So one day he sees a big brick in the garden just below the large window of his father's study. The chemistry is too much for him and suddenly he picks up the brick and heaves it through the window. It's a very bad thing he has done. But the question now is this. Does he go back to the court house to face the judge? Of course the answer has to be no. Why not? Because the judge is now his father. If the judge is a good father he will administer the appropriate little spanking just south of the equator where it makes a difference to naughty youngsters. But he will not send the boy back to the court house to be confronted by the judge. The child is disciplined, if the father is a good one, but not cast out of the family. Why not? Because he has been ransomed, redeemed and adopted.

Thus it is that God decrees a penalty for sin over us and then as judge He pays in His love what He decreed in His justice as Jesus the Son of God comes into the world explaining to the human race that "I have come to give My life a ransom for many" (Matthew 20:28).

So it is on the basis of the death of Christ that we have first been ransomed from our sins and then adopted into the family of God and made by adoption what we are not by nature, namely children of God. Thus the Apostle Paul can write in Romans 8:1: "There is therefore now no condemnation for those who are in Christ Jesus." On that Final Day we will face Him not as judge but as Father. All of this is because of what Jesus did for us on Calvary's Tree.

The metaphor of paying a ransom, particularly to purchase a slave in the ancient slave markets of the first century, also has another suggestive image which goes along with it, namely that of a wealthy master purchasing a slave, not to have the slave work for him, but in order to free the slave and give him his liberty. And gaining our liberty and spiritual freedom through a ransom paid for us by Jesus on the Cross is also very much part of the blessings the New Testament offers us. Says the apostle: "For freedom Christ has set us free; stand fast therefore, and do not submit again to a yoke of slavery" (Galatians 5:1).

Jesus as Testator

A testator of course is one who makes a will and whose inheritance comes to his heirs on his death. In Hebrews 9:15 the writer speaks about our having through Christ an "eternal inheritance" bequeathed to us. Says the writer: "For where a will is involved, the death of one who made it must be established. For a will takes effect only at death, since it is not enforced as long as the one who made it is alive" (Hebrews 9:16-17). Here Jesus is presented as a testator, as one who bequeaths to us an inheritance which becomes valid and operative at the time of His death.

Here then is another marvellous image that through the death of our Lord Jesus Christ an eternal heritance of forgiveness and eternal life is made available to us as heirs. Says Peter in his first epistle (1 Peter 1:3-4): "By His great mercy we have been born anew to a living hope through the resurrection of Jesus Christ from the dead and to an *inheritance* which is imperishable, unde-

filed, unfailing, kept in heaven for you."
How glorious! How wonderful! This extraordinary inheritance of eternal life is made over to us through a new will, and a new covenant. In our Bibles it is called The New Testament.

"It is finished"

On the cross therefore, we have seen, through the metaphors presented above, that Jesus has dealt with human sin, rebellion and alienation. This He has done by taking our sins upon Himself, by giving Himself in love for us, by paying the penalty for our misdemeanours and wrongdoings, by giving His life as a ransom so that we might be set free and finally by bringing into operation a will, a covenant, and a New Testament by which the legacy and inheritance of eternal life is made over to us.

No wonder then that on the cross He could cry out victoriously: "It is finished" (John 19:30). What He had done on the cross represented the complete divine work of atonement, redemption and salvation for the human race. Nothing more needed to be done from God's side. And from our side, there remains no necessity to do anything, because "it is not of works least anyone should boast" (Ephesians 2:8). All we have to do is by faith to receive *something done*. Says the Anglican prayer book: "He made there by His one oblation of Himself once offered, a full, perfect and sufficient sacrifice, oblation and satisfaction for the sins of the whole world."

Our response to the Cross and the Crucified One

First of all, *we have to believe* that He is indeed the Saviour of the world and what He did on Calvary's Tree was for our salvation. We have to believe that He died for our sins and is offering us forgiveness and "the free gift of eternal life" (Romans 6:23).

Secondly, we have to *receive*. In the prologue of John the Apostle writes: "But as many as received Him, as believed in His name, to them He gave authority to become children of God" (John 1:12). We now reach out and receive Him as Saviour and receive what

He has done on our behalf. This we have to do because the cycle of pardon has to be closed by the guilty party rather than the innocent.

Thirdly, we have to *yield or commit* our lives to Christ as Lord and King. This involves a surrendering of ourselves and our wills.

Finally, we are called into discipleship as our Lord Jesus says, "Follow me" (John 1:43).

Perhaps the whole matter of response will become clearer as we move now in our next chapter into the issue of Christian conversion.

10   Chapter Ten

Conversion as the Gateway to Heaven

October 23rd this year, 2005, will be the 50th anniversary of my conversion to Christ. As clearly as if it were yesterday I remember this date in 1955 when my friend Robert Footner led me into Christian commitment to Jesus Christ and showed me how to turn from going my way to going His, which is really what conversion is all about. On that far-off day in a little bed-sitter in Cambridge I opened my heart to Jesus Christ and asked Him to come in to my life by His Holy Spirit and become my Saviour, Lord and Friend.

Personal conversion

As Robert invited me to commit my life to Christ with him then and there, so I knelt in that little bed-sitter and with fumbling faith and stumbling words invited Christ into my heart and attempted to surrender myself to Him.

Robert told me later that he had indeed explained the Cross, but to be honest I don't remember that and certainly, if he did, I did not comprehend it. What I did comprehend, however, was his explanation of Revelation 3:20 where Jesus says: "I stand at the door and knock, if anyone hears My voice, and opens the door, I will come in ... "

Before that day was out I had a sense of the presence of Jesus with me and that I had amazingly entered into a personal knowledge of Him. Suddenly it was just as if I did indeed know Him and He was there and connection had happened. It was awesome. And I knew that I had taken the single most important step that humans are invited to take during the course of their earthly lifetime.

In due course the meaning of the Cross became clearer to me and I understood the central importance of what Jesus did on Calvary's Tree and the spiritual, theological and moral necessity of turning to Him in true conversion.

Thankfully, and most wonderfully, I can indeed say that the adventure over these last 50 years of knowing Christ personally has never, ever been disappointing nor have I ever ceased to be aware of His presence with me. Nor have I ever lost the blessing of knowing that I know Him in a personal way. Not exhaustively or totally, but nevertheless truly. Only when we see Him face to face will that partial knowledge give way to glorious fullness. (1 Corinthians 13:12).

In any event, what I certainly can say is that from October 23rd 1955, life began to change. Indeed the very Sunday following my new Christian commitment, I saw a bulletin board outside a church which carried a quotation from the Apostle Paul found in 2 Corinthians 5:17: "If anyone is in Christ, he is a new creation; old things have passed away, behold all things have become new."

"Goodness gracious", I said to Robert, "even St Paul found what I have found!" And life did indeed begin to change with new and changed attitudes to God, to church, to family and friends as well as to calling, career and service.

Biblical teaching on conversion

Some Scriptural texts

One thing is for sure and that is that the idea of conversion produces much confusion in most people's minds. But it is exceedingly important to know its meaning. After all, Jesus said: "Unless you are converted and become as little children, you will not enter the Kingdom of Heaven" (Matthew 18:3). Entry into the Kingdom of Heaven is here made dependent upon conversion. Who then can afford to ignore what this means and involves? For conversion is here indeed presented as the gateway to heaven and to eternal life.

Not surprisingly then, Scripture's call to humans to repent and be converted is unequivocal. Some 50 Hebrew and some ninety Greek words convey the basic idea of conversion in scripture. The most common Hebrew word is "SHUV" which means to turn, return or to turn back. Thus the Psalmist can say: "The law of the Lord is perfect, converting the soul" (Psalm 19:7). Likewise: "I will teach transgressors Thy ways and sinners will return to Thee" (Psalm 51:13).

In the New Testament the Greek word is *"epistrepho"*. It means to turn from going one direction and then move in another. Thus Jesus can say to Peter: "I have prayed for you that your faith should not fail; when you have turned again, strengthen your brethren" (Luke 22:20). Likewise the Apostle Peter can preach: "Repent and be converted (i.e. turn) that your sins may be blotted out" (Acts 3:19). Other examples of *epistrepho* come in Matthew 13:15, Mark 4:12, John 12:40 and Acts 28:27.

The slightly simpler word *strepho* comes in Matthew 18:3 with Jesus' monumental words: "Unless you turn and become like little children you will never enter the Kingdom of Heaven." Other instructive texts come in 1 Thessalonians 1:19 where it says that some of the Thessalonians *"turned* to God from idols." The Apostle Peter can write: "After straying like sheep, people have 'now returned (or turned) to the Shepherd and Guardian of their souls" (1 Peter 2:25).

The turning from idols and from sin is usually called repentance while the turning to God and to His Christ is usually called faith. So we can say that repentance plus faith equals conversion.

Conversion and regeneration
Conversion and regeneration are obverse and reverse sides of the same coin. Regeneration is God's act (see John 3:5-8), whereas conversion is man's turning to God which meets at once with God's regenerating act. New birth is from above which is the meaning of the Greek word *anothen* used in John 3:7. It is the same word used to describe the veil of the temple being rent "from the top to the bottom." This birth from above has the Holy Spirit as its agent (John 3:6,8). This giving of new birth, this regenerating act, is what God does. However, conversion and turning to Him, is what we

humans do when we repent and believe, even though this too is by grace (e.g. Acts 11:18; 18:27; Ephesians 2:8-9). God's grace enables us to do something, namely to repent, believe and turn, so that we become converted people, in other words people who have turned to the living God.

All of this means that regeneration is unconscious, while conversion is very conscious. At least this is generally so for adults. While some, for example people raised in a Christian home, turn gradually over many years and are in that sense not conscious of conversion at a given moment in time, adult converts can generally point to a moment of conscious conversion, even if they were not necessarily emotionally conscious of God's act of regeneration in them. The results of regeneration, however, are soon experienced in new believers in the sense of new joy, peace, release, power, incentive to witness and so on. Yet the moment of passing from death to life is unconscious.

So then, regeneration is an instantaneous and complete work of God while conversion (repentance plus faith) tends to be more of a process than an event. As with our physical birth, so with new birth, there are months of gestation which may precede it and years of growth which must follow it.

Conversion and repentance
We must register rather sadly that modern calls to conversion often overlook the primacy of repentance, although this was central in Jesus' preaching (e.g. Mark 1:15; Luke 13:3-5) and in that of the apostles (e.g. Acts 2:38; 3:19; 17:30). So in our eagerness to make converts we must not weaken the call to repentance by promising that all things can become new while not insisting that the old things pass away (cf 2 Corinthians 5:17)!

I remember once hearing Billy Graham tell a story of a drunkard who got onto an aeroplane in which he was flying. The man was totally inebriated. His foul language in front of the whole plane was a disgrace, even along with requests to fly the plane plus accompanying acts of flirtation with the stewardesses. A desperate stewardess, hoping this trick would work, told the man that Billy Graham was sitting right behind him. At which point the drunk staggered to his feet, turned slowly around, and holding out his hand said with blurred speech: "Mr Graham, your sermons have really helped me!" To which Billy Graham commented, "I guess he didn't get the bit about repentance!"

The fact is that repentance is integral to conversion. The Greek word most commonly used is *metanoia* meaning literally a change of mind leading to a change of direction. This is what the prodigal son did. He changed his mind about the value of the life he was leading with the pigs, and he decided to change direction and go back to his father. It means seriously coming to Jesus Christ as Lord. Without this no true conversion can be said to have taken place. There may indeed be some psychological experience from superficial acts of turning, but as an authentic renewing experience of the Holy Spirit in conversion, it would be sadly lacking.

This is not to say that Christian conversion does not have its psychological side, because it does, but we must insist that genuine Christian conversion has a uniqueness which is not exhausted by its psychological phenomena.

Conversion and faith
Obviously, faith is an integral component of conversion. Says the writer to the Hebrews: "Without faith it is impossible to please Him. For whoever would draw near to God must believe that He exists, and that He rewards those who seek Him" (Hebrews 11:6).

So what really is faith? In my view, faith is a conviction of the mind plus a commitment of the destiny. This happens, for example, when we marry someone, or get on a plane, or sit on a chair, or submit ourselves to a doctor for an operation. The mind is persuaded that this act of faith commitment and trust is valid, the heart is drawn, and the will is exercised. Faith thus has intellectual, emotional and volitional dimensions to it. I believe in my mind in a person, action or process, and then through my will I commit myself to that person or action.

We can also say that faith is a response of commitment to a sufficiency of evidences. When in our car we crest a hill on a highway, we feel we have an adequacy of evidences that the highway will not suddenly vanish over the edge of a 1000-foot cliff. But we do not at that moment have scientific proof that such could not be the case. But we feel we have enough evidence that the Roads Department of our province is reliable and this enables us to believe that the road goes reliably over the hill and down the other side. Likewise if one goes to a doctor, one may not have scientific proof that the doctor can perform the appendix operation or even that the doctor is for real and not a fake. But we have a sufficiency of evidence to believe that this is indeed a real doctor with real capabilities. So we entrust ourselves to him for the surgery. Likewise as we look at the object of Christian faith, namely our Lord Jesus Christ, we have a sufficiency of evidence (though not scientific proof) of His deity and historical resurrection to respond to Him meaningfully and fully in faith and trust.

So if repentance is a negative forsaking of what is spoiling our lives, then faith is a positive reorientation of our lives around a new centre of gravity, namely our Lord Jesus Christ. And it is this faith in this focus, in other words in Christ (as we see for example in John 3:16), which delivers a person from perishing.

We must also register that as far as faith is concerned, it is its direction which is key and crucial. If I am sick I can put my faith in a doctor or a quack and what will make the difference is the direction of my faith. Putting faith in a quack will not avail for us, whereas putting our faith in a trained doctor will. We can put faith in a piece of string or a piece of nylon rope to swing over a canyon. The direction of faith again will be crucial to the outcome. Trusting in a piece of string will have us jumping to a premature conclusion, whereas putting our faith in the nylon rope will see us safely over to the other side. Faith's direction is critical. So in Christian things. It is through faith in our Lord Jesus Christ and through "faith in His blood" (Romans 3:25) that we are justified. Any other direction for our faith will be futile.

Christian conversion then takes place as we shift our faith from our good works, or our money, or our position, or an erroneous religious belief and place it in Jesus Christ. He is faith's proper focus. He is the One to whom we are converted. And such an act of turning translates us from Satan's power into God's Kingdom (Acts 26:18).

Conversion and the Holy Spirit

That of course is also the point at which the Christian witness will take on board and trust in the supernatural work of the Spirit of God opening up and illuminating the mind of the spiritual enquirer. Says the apostle: "No one can say Jesus is Lord but by the Holy Spirit." (1 Corinthians 12:3) Jesus for His part put it this way: "No one can come to Me unless the Father who sent Me draws him" (John 6:44). In other words, the Holy Spirit is an essential ingredient in the whole converting process. He illumines the mind of the sincere enquirer and without that illumination, fallen humans could not and would not respond and turn in the converting process.

The Scriptures are also clear that we are then sealed with the Holy Spirit at the time of our repentance and conversion (Ephesians 1:13; 1 Corinthians 1:22). We are at that moment indwelt by the Holy Spirit. For example, 1 Corinthians 3:16 presents the apostle's question to the Corinthians: "Do you not know that you are God's temple and God's Spirit dwells in you?" This means that at the time of repentance, conversion and new birth, we have all of the Holy Spirit. He indwells us. The question is whether He has all of us. This is important because our fullness in the Holy Spirit relates to the degree of our surrender to the Spirit. So in this regard we need to say that it is not a case of receiving Jesus at the time of conversion and new birth, and then later on receiving the Holy Spirit. At the time of conversion we are born again through the Holy Spirit and He indwells us. Our fullness in the Spirit then relates to the extent to which He is released in our lives for two purposes, the first being to bring into our lives the fruit of the Spirit (Galatians 5:22-23) and then secondly to enable us to manifest and use the gifts of the Holy Spirit for service, these being well articulated in 1 Corinthians 12, 1 Corinthians 14, plus Romans 12 and Ephesians 4.

Then obviously, thereafter, and throughout our converted lives, we live in daily dependence upon the work of the Holy Spirit within us. As the Holy Spirit enables us to turn and be converted, so He equips and empowers us as converted people to live the Christian life in a credible way.

Types of conversion

It's extremely important at this point to stress that there can be no stereotyping of any one pattern of conversion. In fact, conversions, like hats and people, come in all sorts of different shapes and sizes. This means that it is particularly important not to make our own conversion experience normative.

As I see it in Scripture, there are four different types worth noting, no doubt amongst others.

Gradual

The biblical example here for me would be the Apostle John. He seems to have turned gradually and almost imperceptibly and without any crunching or crisis moments. My wife Carol's experience is rather like that. She is not able to point to a given moment in time when she believes she became converted and turned in faith to Christ. In fact, she can never remember a moment when Jesus was not real to her. And many people raised in Christian homes have a similar experience. It all happens gradually and there is no fixed Damascus Road moment to which they can point. But in no way does this invalidate the authenticity of their conversion. It's just that it happened slowly and gradually.

Crisis

The Apostle Paul is a good illustration of this. On one day he is going in one direction and is busy persecuting and hammering the church. Then suddenly he turns around dramatically after his Damascus Road experience and begins to go in a new direction. It is a right-about-turn. It is crisis, it is sudden, it is overwhelming. In our African Enterprise ministry we have seen many such conversions. Evangelists everywhere would have seen this.

Spasmodic

This may not be a very good word to describe this kind of conversion, but it speaks of those conversions which happen in fits and starts, rather like the Apostle Peter. One day he is affirming strong faith in Jesus, then the next day he is denying his Lord. Then he is coming back once again in repentance, and then once again failing and then yet again needing restoration. Many people have this sort of experience. They definitely want to follow Christ, but all kinds of happenings, difficulties or temptations get in the way. So they keep affirming faith, then denying it and then finally coming back in full and deep conversion.

Crisis at the end of a process
My biblical illustration here would be the Ethiopian eunuch in Acts 8. Here is a man who has been searching for some time. He is religious. He is studying the scriptures. He is definitely a seeker. He is on his way towards meaningful faith. Then suddenly he is faced with Philip the evangelist explaining to him the meaning of Isaiah 53 (which the eunuch was already reading) and preaching to him Jesus. The Ethiopian responds in commitment right away in what one might call a crisis at the end of a process.

Obviously the point to register here is that no one dare make their own experience normative so that we deem the validity of somebody else's conversion whose pattern is different. Clearly the fact is that we can turn either gradually, or in a sudden right about turn, or in fits and starts, or in a sudden crisis at the end of a long process of enquiry. But however it happens, the hard fact remains that we need to have made this turning and we need to be converted to Jesus Christ if we would enter the Kingdom of Heaven. (Matthew 18:3).

Conversion and the maturing of the convert

One of the tragedies of much modern Christian life, particularly in my own continent of Africa, is that many people do become converts to Jesus Christ but fail to go on and become deep disciples. Clearly the turning to Christ is just the beginning, and now a whole process must get underway in terms of growing a convert into a disciple. My late friend and mentor, Bishop Stephen Neill, used to say that a disciple is one who has not only been converted to Christ, but also been converted to both the church and the world.

We have spoken about the conversion to Christ. We need now

to conclude this chapter with some reflections on being converted both to the church and the world.

Conversion to the Church

To turn to Jesus Christ is to turn and come to His people and to the church as His community where both word and sacraments are ministered to believers. Indeed an isolated Christian is a contradiction in terms. Conversion which does not involve incorporation into the visible worshipping and witnessing community of believers is truncated and incomplete.

Coming to the community of Christ is to come to what should be a new and revolutionary lifestyle. This is both exciting and enormously demanding. The new convert, now integrated into the local church, should with fellow believers no longer "adapt themselves to the pattern of this present world", but let their minds be renewed and their whole nature transformed by the Spirit of God (Romans 12:2). So a whole new world and manner of conduct is required of the young convert who is busy becoming a disciple. It means that the world and everything in it has lost both its absolute value and its absolute claim on the new Christian. The young convert is now part of a new, Messianic community which lives by a new value system where its members renounce at the very least the three false values of money, glory and power.

The new convert should also find him or herself in a remarkable new fellowship where differences of race, culture, economic or educational background, have no major significance. This is a fellowship which transcends all natural groupings and leaps over all human barriers. In the first century world, as the Christians manifested this, there was nothing like it anywhere else and there still isn't, even now.

Conversion to the world

The Christian convert turns both from the world and to the world. Conversion must not take the convert out of the world, but send him or her back into it. We do not turn to the world's lifestyle obviously, but we do turn towards the world in its need. So conversion must not take the convert out of the world, but send him or her back into it. The point is that if Jesus's first call was to "come", His second was to "go." In fact, His last words on earth were the Great Commission, exhorting His disciples to go and preach the Gospel to every creature. This being the case, His last words should be our first concern. The Great Commandment is thus followed by the Great Commission. This means that, as Christians, we are gathered in the church only to be dispersed out into the world. The church is therefore not a place of retreat, relaxation and leisure, but the one place where my relaxation and leisure are seriously moderated so that one may go out to help meet the world's demands and needs.

And the first need which the world has is to be evangelised. There are some three billion people who still need to hear and grasp the gospel. A convert has to face that. She cannot be a secret disciple. For either her secrecy will destroy her discipleship, or her discipleship will destroy her secrecy. The convert must share her faith with the world which "God so loved" (John 3:16).

The world, in the second instance, needs to be cared for. This means that the true convert will become caught up in practical ministries of love, compassion and care. These will be evident as the inevitable fruits of a thorough conversion. Thus the thirsty will receive water, the hungry food, the naked clothing. The sick and imprisoned will be visited. (Matthew 25:34-46).

Likewise, the alienated will be brought into reconciliation. For to the converted and reconciled person has been given "the ministry of reconciliation" (2 Corinthians 5:18).

Finally the oppressed and the victims of injustice will find a champion in the truly converted person. For such a person will find a denial of another person's dignity and the restriction of their freedom intolerable.

Summary

Speaking at the South African Congress on Mission and Evangelism back in 1973, Leighton Ford, then on the Billy Graham team, summarised his view of what conversion involved. "Conversion, biblically speaking, is a metaphor of motion. A man is going one way. He stops, turns around, and walks back in the opposite direction. This act of conversion includes what he turns from, what he turns to, and the act of turning itself. To a Christian, conversion is unique in that the turning pivots on the Person of Jesus Christ. Conversion is always a human response to a divine initiative. In the New Testament, men and women are called to turn to God because 'the Kingdom of God is at hand' (Mark 1:15). This means that God has brought history to a climax in the arrival of Jesus Christ. God raised up Jesus, whom men crucified, showing Him to be Lord and Christ, exalting Him and through Him sending the Holy Spirit. This good news of a new era and a new life demands decision. Conversion therefore is far more than an isolated religious or emotional experience. It is a complete reorientation of the personality towards a new centre as a result of a real personal encounter with Jesus Christ. It is nothing less than becoming a part of God's new creation in Christ."[62]

"For if anyone be in Christ, they are a new creation: Old things have passed away. Behold all things have become new" (2 Corinthians 5:17).

Chapter Eleven

The Person and Work of the Holy Spirit

If coming to grips with the Person of Jesus Christ takes us to the heart of things in the Christian faith, then personally entering into the work of the Holy Spirit takes us in even deeper.

But the issue is not straightforward, as I have shared in my book on the Holy Spirit, *Bursting the Wineskins*. I am therefore now going to draw primarily from that earlier volume for the substance of what I want to share here.[63]

As I do so, I want to stress that it is important to approach our theological formulations, especially on such a grand theme, with humility, flexibility and grace. How foolish to dare to present a final or definitive word on the Holy Spirit! For our God is God the surpriser, God the unpredictable, God the iconoclast, God the box-breaker, God the de-systematiser of systematic theologians. Much of the current confusion on the Person and work of the Holy Spirit lies in just this – that we have tried to systematise One who is extraordinarily unsystematic. We have tried to confine in neat theological categories One who, like the wind, blows where He wishes, unfettered by the theological formulations in which we seek to contain Him, or the human predictables by which we hope to anticipate Him. In my library, I have dozens of books by authors – orthodox, neo-orthodox and unorthodox, as well as Pentecostal, neo-Pentecostal, anti-Pentecostal – all presenting, equally dogmatically, the definitive word on the Spirit's Person and work! Every one, I suspect, has some of the truth. No one has it all.

Dangers and difficulties

I can see three dangers in most of these books on the Holy Spirit. We may:

1. Talk a lot of theory about the Spirit without letting Him disturb our lives in any significant or creative way.
2. Simply give up on the subject and say it is all too confusing and therefore push it to the edge of our lives and thinking.
3. Hungrily pursue an emotional experience of the Spirit on which we then build a theology regardless of the Bible's teaching, without struggling with the New Testament data.

Dangers one and two (academic theologising on the one hand and intellectual despairing on the other) leave our lives impoverished. Danger three (theologising on experience) leaves our theology unbalanced. However, neither the danger of dogmatising nor the impossibility of finalising our view of the Spirit's work must make us retreat from an honest attempt to understand the biblical data and apply it to our lives. After all, we don't tolerate such retreats when it comes to the Bible's teaching on the atonement or on conversion or on prayer, so nor can we tolerate such a retreat from the Bible's view of the Holy Spirit. Rather, in formulating our view we need to do so with humility and flexibility, trying to distinguish between those areas where real clarity is possible and those areas where differences of viewpoint will remain and where a measure of agnosticism is necessary.

Procedure

Different sectors of the Church of course have different approaches to the text of the Bible as they seek to determine their views. Some build their theology of the Spirit just from the distinctly theological sections of the New Testament (e.g., the Gospels and Epistles), charismatics and Pentecostals build theirs more on the historical sections of the New Testament (e.g., the book of Acts).

However, most evangelicals believe it to be an important principle of interpretation that theology is built on theological rather than historical sections of the text. History illustrates doctrine rather than constituting it, at least in any primary sense, we say, though there is an obvious interplay. In other words, we start with theology and end with practice, not vice versa. Put differently, we could say we are to move from the general to the specific, from the systematic to the historical, from doctrine, as found in the Gospels but especially in the Epistles, to the historical outworking of it, as found in the book of Acts. Pentecostals and charismatics, on the other hand, are less persuaded of this as a rigid principle of interpretation and are therefore less squeamish about drawing their theology from the book of Acts.

Perhaps a little give-and-take from each side would be useful. We must ask evangelicals who press this so-called hermeneutical principle to avoid doing so too rigidly. After all, Paul asserted in 2 Timothy 3:16 that "All Scripture is inspired by God and profitable for teaching" (i.e. *all* Scripture – not just doctrinal sections). In the Old Testament, historical sections and prophetic sections are intertwined. In the New Testament, history and teaching are certainly profoundly interrelated in the Gospels. So we must be careful not to apply this principle too artificially. On the other hand, charismatics and Pentecostals need to exercise caution in their use of Acts, particularly if their handling of Acts lands them in doctrinal formulations that are hard to square with the systematic doctrinal statements of the Epistles. We commented on this in chapter 6. Nowhere is this more classically seen than in the controversy surrounding the phenomenon of "the baptism in the Holy Spirit." The Epistles do not speak of any two-tier or double-staged process of initiation into the Christian life, but the book of Acts in places seems to suggest this.

Anyway, the first key item on the agenda is to ask who exactly is the Holy Spirit?

Who is the Holy Spirit?

The Holy Spirit is a person. He is not an "it", not an impersonal influence. Jesus used the masculine pronoun "He" when referring to the Holy Spirit (e.g. John 14:26; 15:26; 16:8,13,14). Moreover, Scripture assigns personal attributes to the Holy Spirit in speaking of His mind, as when He will "teach you all things" (John 14:26); His emotions, as when He "grieves" (Ephesians 4:30) and His will, as when He "forbids" (Acts 16:6-7).

The Holy Spirit is God. He is co-equal with the Father and the Son and proceeds from both Father and Son, as affirmed in the Nicene Creed. Article V of the Anglican Church's Thirty-Nine Articles speaks of Him as "of one substance, majesty and glory with the Father and the Son." Jesus sent His servants out to make disciples and baptise them in the one name "of the Father and of the Son and of the Holy Spirit" (Matthew 28:19). The Apostle Paul commended people to "the grace of our Lord Jesus Christ and the love of God and the fellowship of the Holy Spirit" (2 Corinthians 13:14).

The Holy Spirit is the Spirit of Jesus. Throughout the New Testament, and certainly from Acts to Revelation, the Holy Spirit is seen as the Spirit of Jesus. Jesus said, "I tell you the truth: it is to your advantage that I go away, for if I do not go away, the Counsellor will not come to you; but if I go, I will send Him to you" (John 16:7). As the Father had sent Jesus into the world, so Jesus would send the Spirit. The Father would share in that sending but the Spirit would be sent in the name of Jesus. Thus John reported Jesus' words, "But the Counsellor, the Holy Spirit, whom the Father will send in My name, He will teach you all things" (John 14:26). In other words, the Holy Spirit was able to universalise the presence of Jesus. The disciples had perhaps sensed the Spirit with them during the earthly ministry of Jesus, but after the Resurrection they could know Him in them. To His disciples, Jesus said of the Spirit of truth, "you know Him, for He dwells with you, and will be in you" (John 14:17). The Spirit makes it possible for the presence of Jesus to be in the hearts of His disciples everywhere. He cannot be localised, as Jesus had to be in His earthly ministry.

The Spirit does not exist to glorify Himself but to glorify Christ. "He will bear witness to me," Jesus said (John 15:26). The Spirit is like a person operating a movie projector. He projects not Himself but the movie. So the Holy Spirit is not there primarily to give us an experience and knowledge of Himself, but of Christ. That fact gives a certain objectivity and identity to the Spirit's work. For example, seeking after mere spiritual experiences makes for dangerous sentimentality and emotionalism. Christians seek the knowledge and experience of the Spirit of Jesus, which will build them into a greater likeness to Him. Indeed, any "spiritual" experience that does not result in greater likeness to Christ is suspect, because the Spirit, whom we should be seeking or releasing, is the Spirit of Jesus. Therefore, only one thing gives evidence that we have received the Holy Spirit of the Bible, namely our gradually becoming like Jesus (Galatians 5:22-3) and desiring to bring people to Jesus (Acts 1:8).

The Holy Spirit has a threefold ministry in the lives of those who become followers of Jesus – as they seek, believe and follow. Thus the Holy Spirit works in us *before conversion* when He illumines the minds of seekers (1 Corinthians 12:3) and convicts them of their sin and need of a Saviour (John 16:8). He works in us *at conversion* when He regenerates (John 3:5-6) and then indwells the lives of believers (Romans 8:9-10; 1 Corinthians 3:16; 2 Corinthians 1:22) and finally seals them as purchased possessions (Ephesians 1:13). And He works in us *after conversion* when He sanctifies disciples (1 Thessalonians 4:7-8; 1 Corinthians 6:19-20), guides them (John 16:13), helps them to pray (Romans 8:26-27), strengthens them (Ephesians 3:16), brings forth His fruit (Galatians 5:22-23) and equips them for service through His gifts (1 Corinthians 12:4-11).

All this is part of what the Bible calls "Sanctification". It is a theme of such importance as to require that we devote our next chapter to it.

But for the moment we are focussing on the fullness of the Spirit.

The fullness of the Holy Spirit

The Bible commands us to "be filled with the Spirit" (Ephesians 5:18). This is not a desirable spiritual option but a clear biblical command. If I received the Holy Spirit when I was born again, as I believe I did, and if He indwells me, as I believe He does, then

Paul's exhortation must mean something like this: "You have the Spirit, but does He have you? You have taken Him into your life, but you must now allow Him to fill you – in the sense of releasing yourself to Him so that He can occupy and control every area, every corner, of your being."

When we are born again, it is as if God by His Spirit lands on alien occupied territory. Then He must be allowed to advance from that "beachhead" to occupy and fill all the territory with His presence and rule. This is the process of *sanctification*, the advance of Jesus the King and of His Kingdom or kingship in our lives. In many ways this must, of necessity, be a lifetime matter, but sometimes God may make an extremely dramatic breakthrough when all at once we allow Him by our surrender, to capture massive and hitherto unsurrendered tracts of our lives. At such moments we may experience overwhelming joy, release, power and praise.

We must also recognise another important truth that is especially brought home in Paul's epistles: *in Christ the believer has already been blessed with all spiritual blessings*. Thus the Apostle can say, "Blessed be the God and Father of our Lord Jesus Christ, who has blessed us in Christ with every spiritual blessing in the heavenly places" (Ephesians 1:3). In other words, if we are in Christ, every spiritual blessing is already potentially ours. It is all reckoned to our account. It is our possession and we "have come to fullness of life in Him" (Colossians 2:10). But we must appropriate our heritage, our rightful inheritance. Most of us do not do that and as a result we seriously impoverish ourselves.

Thus it is that *our fullness in the Holy Spirit is in proportion to the degree of our surrender*. We are as full of the Holy Spirit as our commitment permits. Disobedience can both "quench the Spirit" (1 Thessalonians 5:19) and "grieve" Him (Ephesians 4:30). We do this when we fail to allow Him to do in us that for which He has been given to us. We can also say that a person who is filled with the Spirit is a person in whose life the fruit of the Spirit is evident (Galatians 5:22-23) and the ministries of the Spirit operative (1 Corinthians 12:4-14). The key evidence of fullness is moral rather than overtly miraculous. It is something more evident to observers of one's life and ministry than to the person who is filled. No one in

Scripture ever claimed to be filled with the Spirit.

Crisis infilling

I would not want, however, to deny the validity of the "crisis infilling" when, sick of ourselves, our sin and our anaemia, we again cast ourselves on Christ with a cry for the infilling, anointing and visitation of His Spirit. That is when God in His faithfulness may come upon us or be released in us in power, sometimes with and sometimes without the accompanying gift of tongues, but always with joy and release.

On this, most of us can agree. And would we not all agree with A.W. Tozer and his observation: "Satan has opposed the doctrine of the Spirit-filled life about as bitterly as any doctrine there is. He has confused it, opposed it, surrounded it with false notions and fears. He has blocked every effort of the Church of Christ to receive from the Father her divine and blood-bought patrimony. The Church has tragically neglected this great liberating truth – that there is now for the child of God a full and wonderful and completely satisfying anointing with the Holy Spirit. The Spirit-filled life is not a special, deluxe edition of Christianity. It is part and parcel of the total plan of God for His people."[64]

Unquestionably, multitudes of believers feel that somewhere along the line they have entered some such experience, some in charismatic or Pentecostal settings and some not. Inevitably there are varying understandings and labels. Some call it a "second blessing". Others call it "crisis sanctification" or "the filling with the Spirit" or "the release of the Spirit" or the "baptism in the Spirit".

The term "filled with the Spirit" (Ephesians 5:18) or "full of the Spirit" (Acts 6:3) regularly occurs in Scripture and seems best to describe the experience we are talking about. It also seems to be the term the greatest number of people can live with amicably as the preferred term. It can fit either the once-for-all, non-repeatable experience or the ongoing experience of appropriation, rededication and refilling. Certainly those holding this view should not oppose others who attach a different label to the same reality, for example, "baptism in the Spirit". The Holy Spirit Himself, I am sure, is not so fussed about labels as perhaps we are. All He wants is to fill us and control us, regardless of what name or label we attach to this very special blessing.

Most especially does He want to see us become not only holy and more like Christ, but equipped to serve Him effectively.

Chapter Twelve

Sanctification – Growing in the Christian Life

The Holy Spirit, we must remember, is the *Holy* Spirit. As such, it is His special role to work on making the believer *holy*. This also includes the notion of "wholeness" – and "set-apartness". We are made whole, we are "set apart" for the Lord's service. We are also to be equipped for it.

Sanctification is the name of the process that is begun at conversion and made possible by justification. Sanctification, notes Baptist theologian, Augustus Strong, "is that continuous operation of the Holy Spirit, by which the holy disposition imparted in regeneration [i.e. new birth] is maintained and strengthened."[65] It is important to note that, in justification, we are pronounced innocent by God on the basis of our trust in the atoning death of Jesus on the Cross for our sins. That is where the basis of our salvation lies. It depends on God "justifiying" us.

On the other hand, our salvation does not in essence depend upon our sanctification. Nonetheless, it is of crucial importance for the Christian. Sanctification envelops both the meaning and the pilgrimage of the Christian's life. The 16th century English admiral and navigator, Sir Francis Drake, captured sanctification's importance in his famous prayer, "Lord, teach me, when I endeavour any great matter, that it is not the beginning, but the continuing of the same until it has been thoroughly finished which yields the true glory." Paul saw sanctification as critical and tells Timothy to "be diligent in these matters; give yourself wholly to them, so that everyone may see your progress" (I Timothy 4:15).

Separate

While sanctification must be preceded by justification, they are distinctly separate ideas. *Justification* deals with whether or not we are forgiven. It addresses our judicial relationship with God (whether we are seen as innocent or guilty) and it is based on a righteousness that is *imputed*. It is the foundation of our peace and security in Christ. It guarantees that our acceptance by God is complete, perfect and final, sudden and once for all. *Sanctification*, by contrast, is God's righteousness *imparted*. It concerns our state of being and our spiritual fellowship with the Father and with others. It shows the progress in our morality and holiness before God and in our efforts to attain Christian character. And it is a gradual process. Sanctification, as noted, has no causal relationship to the salvation of the believer, but is the result of our ongoing relationship with Christ. Justification is a single act of the Father coming to us by grace through faith as we receive the Son as Saviour and Lord. Sanctification is the gradual process of the Holy Spirit dealing with our old nature over our whole lifetime.

Practical

The very term "sanctification" could make our discussion of this vital process sound abstract or theoretical, but it is actually very practical. This becomes evident as we think of the means by which we can grow in Christ.

We should read our Bibles. Paul, in 2 Timothy 2:15 urges us to, "Do your best to present yourself to God as one approved, a workman who has no need to be ashamed, rightly handling the word of truth."

We should pray daily. Oswald Chambers affirms that prayer is our life's work and nothing is more important. The whole Bible affirms this.

We should be constantly engaged in Christian fellowship. Friendships with non-Christians should certainly be nurtured and maintained, but if we do not build significant relationships with Christians and involve ourselves in the Church, we deprive ourselves of a vital dimension of Christian life and means of growth.

We must share our faith with others (i.e. witness). In fact, if we are not willing to pin our colours to the mast, then we go directly against an oft-repeated scriptural mandate. For example, Paul states "if you confess with your lips that Jesus is Lord and believe in your heart that God raised Him from the dead, you will be saved" (Romans 10:9). In fact, "every one who calls upon the name of the Lord will be saved. But how are men to call upon Him in whom they have not believed? And how are they to believe in Him of whom they have never heard? And how are they to hear without a preacher?" (Romans 10:13,14) All this means that a secret disciple is a contradiction in terms. For either our discipleship destroys our secrecy or our secrecy destroys our discipleship.

There is our regular involvement in the sacrament of the Lord's Supper or Holy Communion. As New Testament baptism, like Old Testament circumcision, opens the way to fellowship in the visible household of faith (though we do not hold with baptismal regeneration), so sharing in the Lord's Supper allows us to be spiritually fed in a deep and powerful way in fellowship with other believers. Whoever would grow in Christ, therefore, shares in the Lord's Supper regularly as a memorial of His death and passion and remembers the Lord's death until He comes again.

We must be willing to allow Jesus Christ to attain lordship over the whole of our life. Romans 14:9 states that, "For to this end Christ died and lived again, that He might be the Lord both of the dead and of the living." W.H. Griffith Thomas says: "the 'absolute monarchy' of Jesus Christ is the one condition of genuine Christian living."[66] In today's world, proclaiming the rights of the individual and freedom for all is far better received than talking about servanthood, even servanthood to God. Yet, it is in this servanthood that we finally find true meaning and joy in life.

Separated and set apart

All the practical steps just mentioned lead on to the fulfilment of the intention of the original Hebrew word for holiness. This means being used for a special (religious) purpose or function and in particular to be set apart for God. The idea of being separated for a holy use can be traced back to Moses, who at God's command, "sanctified" all the Hebrew first-born. Thus Aaron and his sons were "sanctified" to minister to God in the priest's office and Israel as a nation was "set apart" as God's chosen people. Indeed, those who have been set apart by God are obliged to sanctify themselves, or to separate themselves from all that defiles. Quite a challenge!

Our role in sanctification then, is not only to pursue holiness actively through reading the Bible, prayer, witness, the sacraments etc., but also to avoid evil influences and be set apart from them as far as possible. Such a task can be difficult in this day of omnipresent smut, immorality and the ungodly media. But in all of this we must remember that the Lord, not us, is the primary actor in the universe and it is the blood of Christ that must be relied upon to set us apart. Beyond that, there is the Holy Spirit who is the great sanctifier and who empowers us as we try to keep ourselves clear of evil. Because of the work of these two persons of the Trinity, we become cleansed vessels in the new, spiritual temple and ready for the Master's use.

Spiritual gifts

As believers press on in the journey of sanctification and are set apart for God to an ever-greater degree, spiritual gifts begin to manifest themselves more and more clearly. Spiritual gifts, or gifts of the Holy Spirit, are supernatural endowments that enable us to do what we otherwise could not do. I always find it encouraging to register that every believer is endowed with spiritual gifts. So Paul can affirm that, "To *each* is given the manifestation of the Spirit for the common good" (1 Corinthians 12:7). But to a certain extent it is up to us to develop the gifts that we have been given. We are likewise instructed to "Make love your aim, and earnestly desire the spiritual gifts" (1 Corinthians 14:1). So it is not love or gifts but love *and* gifts.

According to Scripture, various spiritual gifts enable and equip us to do a variety of things. These include, among others, the ability to teach, preach, prophesy, speak in tongues, administer, counsel, heal, help and lead. Wisdom, knowledge and faith are also tied to the gifts of the Holy Spirit (1 Corinthians 12:8-10).[67] Every one of these gifts and others is vital to healthy congregational life and also the strengthening of the individual's faith. All this makes the Church more effective in its ministry as a whole. If believers used their spiritual gifts in an effective manner, the way would open to our growing up in many exciting new ways and being a community of hope and a people of love able to influence deeply the world around us.[68]

Integral to the proper use of spiritual gifts is the Lord's very demanding way of love. Paul reminds us of this by using his three famous zeros in 1 Corinthians 13:1-3: "If I speak in the tongues of men and of angels, but have not love, I am a noisy gong or a clanging cymbal (= zero 1). And if I have prophetic powers, and understand all mysteries and all knowledge, and if I have all faith, so as to remove mountains, but have not love, I am nothing (= zero 2). If I give away all I have, and if I deliver my body to be burned, but have not love, I gain nothing" (= zero 3). So love becomes what Studdert Kennedy once called the *summum bonum* or highest good of the Christian life. It is also the most "gutsy" and demanding assignment to fulfil and all of us fail here constantly. Even so, it remains true that without a genuine love and concern for people, our spiritual gifts will be empty and fleshly and of little benefit, as Paul had to reiterate constantly to the very charismatic Corinthians!

Faith and sanctification

Because the term "justification by faith" has become standard phraseology, it is normal to link the two words together. However, we must not forget the crucial relationship between faith and sanctification. The process of sanctification is, in many ways, simply the deepening of the Christian's faith, which allows us to walk more and more in step with the Lord and glorify Him more fully. Strong writes that, "though the weakest faith perfectly justifies, the degree of sanctification is measured by the strength of the Christian's faith, and the persistence with which he or she apprehends Christ."[69]

The famous eleventh chapter of Hebrews provides a clear picture of what strong faith can accomplish. The sixth verse says "without faith it is impossible to please Him. For whoever would draw near to God must believe He exists and that He rewards those who seek Him." The passage that follows verse 6 provides some amazing insights on how mature faith behaves. In verse 8, for example, faith *obeys* and *follows* when it hears the voice of God. "By faith Abraham obeyed ... and went out, not knowing where he was to go." Faith also sees and copes with the "not yet". In verse 10 Abraham looked forward to a city with deep spiritual foundations. At that time there was nothing in sight, yet eventually the nation of Israel would dwell on the land upon which he gazed.

Faith will also make sacrifices, as is evidenced when Abraham did not hesitate to put his own son on the altar (v. 17). Further characteristics of mature faith include the securing of blessings for the future (v. 20), perseverance (v. 27), the crossing of the Red Sea (v. 29) and the making of walls to fall down (v. 30). All of these things were made possible through ordinary people with extraordinary faith and deep sanctification. It would be quite exciting indeed if the faith of believers today could mature to the point where we could achieve and bring forth these sorts of staggering results.

Pilgrims

In the Christian walk nothing comes quickly or easily, which is why the pilgrim analogy has so often been used to describe it and also the sanctification process. Augustine centred his most important work, *The City of God*, around this analogy as he explained that Christians are not citizens of the earthly city only, but most especially are pilgrims journeying through this world to another destination, the City of God. That is where our citizenship is really established. John Bunyan used this same theme over 1,000 years later in writing *The Pilgrim's Progress*. Bunyan's heroes, Hopeful and Faithful, had many trying adventures as they made their way through the earthly city. In fact, Faithful's pilgrimage was cut short at Vanity Fair where he was burned at the stake, leaving Hopeful to continue alone. Had he stayed in Vanity Fair or any other stop along the way, his Christian life would have stopped progressing. This is true in the sanctification process of all Christians. Physical and mental growth is what we normally anticipate for everyone, but sadly this rule does not apply to our spiritual growth. Thus Paul could tell the Corinthians in 1 Corinthians 3:1, "But I, brethren, could not address you as spiritual men, but as men of the flesh, as babes in Christ." Although addressing adults, many of whom have been Christians for some time, he still sees them as "babes in Christ". Immature Christians often act like ordinary people or citizens of the earthly city. For Paul, the most damning indictment on some Christians is that they are "behaving like *ordinary* men" (1 Corinthians 3:3). To be "ordinary" is to become a "settler" living life on earth in a purely earthly way and without proper reference to the Spirit's control and guidance.

Being a settler is not simply a neutral state of nongrowth, but also has actively negative aspects. The consequence of not growing up into Christian maturity is that not only do we not bring into the Church the blessings of the spiritual person's life, but we plague the Church and ourselves with the curses of the fleshly life, as listed in Galatians 5:19-21: immorality, impurity, licentiousness, factiousness, idolatry and strife, to name just a few. If too many become settlers in the Church rather than pilgrims growing in holiness and spirituality, we destroy the Church's credibility and endanger its ministry.

Summary

Let us remember that sanctification is a process that springs out of the conversion experience and is made possible through our justification by grace through faith. The Christian's ultimate goal in sanctification, as Thomas á Kempis affirmed, is the *Imitation of Christ*. Such a goal is of course, not fully attainable in this life due to the stubborn resistance of our "old natures". Thankfully however, the Holy Spirit is engaged in renewing and purifying us toward levels of Christlikeness, which no one could even remotely achieve without supernatural assistance. As this renewal progresses, we become set apart for God's glory, much as the nation of Israel was set apart as we see in the Old Testament.

As Christians make their way down the road of sanctification, their own faith is deepened, the love of Jesus becomes more evident and the gifts of the Spirit are manifested much more clearly and decisively. Sanctification is certainly no easy venture and trials and tribulations, flops and failures will be the lot of all of us all along the way. But actually, it is these trials, failures and hardships that provide the Christian with opportunities to grow in Christ.

John Bunyan (1628-1688) in one of his hymns, describes well the perseverance we must have and the edification that flows from these trials:

He who would valiant be
'Gainst all disaster,
Let him in constancy
Follow the Master.
There's no discouragement
Shall make him once relent
His first avowed intent
To be a pilgrim.

May we all hang in on the bumpy and difficult pilgrim path to godly living for our Lord Jesus Christ.

13

Chapter Thirteen

Defending and Declaring the Truth – Apologetics and Truth

In talking about the Holy Spirit in the last chapter, we did not really get into one of the key ministries of the Holy Spirit in us – namely to make us witnesses to Jesus Christ. Said Jesus: "You shall receive power when the Holy Spirit has come upon you and you shall be My witnesses in Jerusalem, Judaea and to the ends of the earth" (Acts 1:6). Now a witness is one who points to Christ, who testifies to the truth of the Gospel and who will seek at every opportunity, whether in private or public, to defend the Gospel. Also to give "a reason" for the belief we have. Says Peter: "Always be ready to give a defence [reason] for the hope that is in you" (1 Peter 3:15).

The Greek word for "reason" is *apologia* from which we get the English word "apology", but more specifically the more accurate term "apologist" – i.e. one who defends something. So the Christian apologist is one who defends the Christian faith. The developed theological discipline of this is called "Apologetics".

Needless to say, it is vital in our modern times, when so much Christian truth is under attack, to have good Christian apologists.

A great Christian apologist

As I have already stated, one of the most outstanding of these was C.S. Lewis, to whose thought we have had some modest introduction in an earlier chapter.

But now I want to return to him in greater depth in these next couple of chapters and to some of his thought as presented in the *Oxbridge '98* conference to which we have already alluded.

As a Christian apologist (i.e. one giving a reason for Christianity being true), C.S. Lewis was deeply devoted to the pursuit of truth. He would therefore, have been horrified with the contemporary Postmodernist notion (see chapters 16 and 17) that ideas of truth, validity or right reason should no longer be held crucial and that we cannot achieve an accurate "real-world match" between objects, realities or states of affairs and our concepts of understanding, thought or our verbal description of them. Likewise that we cannot really make truth statements, but only express "opinions".

Anticipating the contemporary situation

Perhaps however, Lewis was anticipating our contemporary situation, where truth statements are declared either impossible or irrelevant. His character, Screwtape (the devil), advises Wormwood (a junior devil) to keep argument and questions of "true or false" away from his patient's mind, the patient being someone Wormwood was trying to prevent from coming to Christian faith.

In fact, Screwtape celebrates that while in the past humans pretty much knew and were concerned with whether things were true and proven or not, Wormwood needs to focus on keeping his patient content with having "a dozen incompatible philosophies dancing together in his head" without letting him ask, let alone discover, which were true and which were false. Rather, he must keep the patient lazily languishing in notions of "meaningfulness" or "practical helpfulness" or "being contemporary". He must keep him tolerant of everything and whatever happens, keep him away from notions of truth or falsity!

But I am getting ahead of myself, so we need to backtrack and see:

- How C.S. Lewis understood apologetics.
- How he viewed truth and the phenomenon of facts.
- What he felt he should defend as "true" in Christianity.

How Lewis understood apologetics

At *Oxbridge '98*, numbers of C.S. Lewis' old friends were present. These and other friends once combined to issue a volume called *Light on C.S. Lewis*, a fascinating volume in which there is a fine essay on "The Christian Apologist" by Austen Farrer, the foremost Oxford theologian of his day and also a close friend of Lewis. In it, Farrer notes a Lewis conviction that while "rational argument is so seldom the cause of Christian conviction", nevertheless "the lack of it destroys belief. What seems to be proved may not be embraced" (i.e. by sceptics), yet "what no one shows the ability to defend is quickly abandoned. Rational argument does not of itself create belief, but it does maintain a climate in which belief may flourish. So the apologist who does nothing but defend may play a useful, though preparatory, part."[70]

In other words, while our arguments or apologetics, as used to demonstrate the truth of Christian faith, will not in and of themselves bring people to Christian commitment (the Holy Spirit does that – 1 Corinthians 12:3), nevertheless if what we are proclaiming is historically, factually or intellectually indefensible (i.e. it is not true), then we are not only deceiving others, but ourselves, and the whole missionary and evangelistic enterprise is both a sham and a shame.

What we are to defend and proclaim as apologists, is that all of life makes sense in Christ and the Gospel facts and realities, and in no other way.

Timeless in modern dress

Lewis says this can only be achieved by the biblical apologist who maintains a "detachment from passing fashions"[71] along with a refusal on principle to be a sort of chameleon which adjusts its colour to the environment of the moment. "Our business is to present that which is timeless (the same yesterday, today and tomorrow) in the particular language of our own age. The bad preacher does exactly the opposite: he takes the ideas of our own age and tricks them out in the traditional language of Christianity … Your teaching must be timeless at its heart but wear a modern dress."[72]

In a talk in Wales in 1945 on "Christian Apologetics", this kind of conviction also led Lewis to warn a group of ministers and would-be apologists about drifting into accommodating positions which supposedly make defending the faith easier (e.g. by removing supernaturalism).

However, in effect these are a departure from the "faith once for all delivered to the saints", that is, from the timeless heart of New Testament Christianity.

Lewis notes that "our upbringing and the whole atmosphere of the world we live in make it certain that our main temptation will be that of yielding to winds of doctrine, not that of ignoring them. We are not at all likely to be hidebound; we are very likely indeed to be the slaves of fashion…The standard of permanent Christianity must be kept clear in our minds and it is against that standard that we must test all contemporary thought. In fact, we must at all costs *not* move with the times. We serve One who said, 'Heaven and Earth shall move with the times, but My words shall not move with the times.'"[73]

The fact is that when key aspects of biblical supernaturalism are lost, then in effect one has "become so broad or liberal or modern" that one "ceases to be Christian at all." If that happens, Lewis said to the ministers, "you must change your profession." I agree and I think most laity in the Church would also agree.

For example, certain bishops and other Church leaders in both the United Kingdom and the United States are happy to express publicly a basic denial of the historic Christian faith. They are, of course, at liberty to do so and no doubt their problems are genuine, but they should not be bishops or Church leaders or paid by the Church for propagating that which bears little if any resemblance to biblical Christianity. Apart from anything else, they hugely complicate the labours of genuine preachers, apologists, ministers and evangelists.

Listen again to Lewis as he proceeds to urge those ministers who deny the faith, while purporting to defend it, to change their profession: "This is your duty not specially as Christians or as priests but as honest men. There is a danger here of the clergy developing a special professional conscience which obscures the very plain moral issue. Men who have passed beyond proper boundary lines are apt to protest that they have come by their unorthodox opinions honestly. In defence of these opinions they are prepared to suffer obloquy (i.e. being ill spoken of) and to forfeit professional advancement. They thus come to feel like martyrs.

"But this simply misses the point which so gravely scandalises the layman. We never doubted that the unorthodox opinions were honestly held; what we complain of is your continuing your ministry after you have come to hold them. We always knew that a man who makes his living as a paid agent of the Conservative Party may honestly change his views and honestly become a Communist. What we deny is that he can honestly continue to be a Conservative agent and to receive money from one party while he supports the policy of another."

Lewis then adds, "Even when we have thus ruled out teaching which is in direct contradiction to our profession, we must define our task still further. We are to defend Christianity itself – the faith preached by the Apostles, attested by the martyrs, embodied in the creeds and expounded by the fathers. This must be clearly distinguished from the whole of what any one of us may think about God and Man.

"Each of us has his individual emphasis, each holds, in addition to the faith, many opinions which seem to him or her to be consistent with it and true and important. And so perhaps they are. But as apologists it is not our business to defend *them*. When we mention our personal opinions we must always make quite clear the difference between them and the faith itself."[74]

Here then is C.S. Lewis, the Christian apologist. We must now press on to how he viewed truth and facts.

How Lewis viewed truth and facts

Lewis held to what has traditionally been called "The Correspondence Theory of Truth". Commenting on this, University of Southern California philosophy professor Dallas Willard noted at *Oxbridge '98*, "In other words, he held that truth is a matter of a belief or an idea corresponding to reality. In the course of rejecting the view that moral laws are social conventions, he insists that they are, on the contrary (and this is the language he uses) 'real truths'.

"He says, 'If your moral ideas can be truer than those of the Nazi, there must be something, some real morality, for them to be true about. The reason that your idea of New York can be truer or less true than mine, is that New York is a real place existing quite apart from what either of us thinks. If when each of us said 'New York', each meant merely the town I am imagining in my own head, how could one of us have truer ideas than the other? There would be no question of truth or falsehood at all.' That is a very characteristic statement of what truth as correspondence means. And you have to understand that it is truth as correspondence that provides what sometimes among philosophers today is called 'the reality-hook' – the connection to reality."

Willard acknowledges that this concept is under attack ("in the fire") today with "the popular assumptions against real truth". The fact is that truth, goodness and beauty are often today seen as "sentimental" and not "objective" – i.e. not independent of the attitude we take towards them. To think otherwise is now "uncool!" said Willard. He went on to suggest trying that line on something unreal and untrue (for example, Pegasus, the winged horse of Greek mythology) and then on something real and true like running out of petrol on a lonely freeway. In the case of Pegasus, we know that it does not exist. "What does that mean? It means simply that the relevant properties that we associate with Pegasus do not together belong to anything. Wingedness and horsiness do not together belong to anything. If they did, that thing would be Pegasus and Pegasus would actually exist."

Clearly, then, "being a fact has nothing to do in general with being thought of or being mentioned or being described." Pegasus can be thought of, even thought of as real or as a fact, but that view is mistaken. It is not real, it is untrue.

Or take the empty petrol tank in our car. "If you assume or believe your car is well supplied with gasoline when it is not, you may find yourself in great danger or discomfort. And this is true even for a Postmodernist or a relativist. When you believe in or trust a crooked or incompetent financial adviser, you may wind up depending upon your relatives or the state and kiss your golden years goodbye. We take seriously how things or facts are. We do not say, 'Oh well, since you believed there was gas in the tank it shall be so.' The truth is," said Willard, that "facts are totally unforgiving."

Likewise "a universe just like ours, except *devoid* of conscious beings and their language, would still be a universe of true facts and existence." In other words, denying the existence of the universe (or else not being there at all to describe it in words) will not remove its truth and factualness, any more than denying the resurrection of Jesus will change it from being true and corresponding to historical reality on a one-to-one ratio, as per Christian conviction. It is not our brains or description which make the universe or the resurrection true or factual. Their truth and factualness precede our perception of them as such. Thus we register that when Christians say, "Jesus is Lord of the Universe", the statement for us is either true or false. Either it honours and accords with reality or it does not. And Christians believe it holds true regardless of anyone's opinion on the subject, truth not being determined by subjective views, majority votes or cultural fashions. For example, it is true and a fact that the world was spherical even when the majority vote of the early Middle Ages said it was flat!

This is the correspondence view of truth, held also by the Apostle Paul. He said, "if Christ has not been raised, then our preaching is in vain and your faith is in vain. We are even found to be misrepresenting God, because we testified of God that He raised Christ, whom He did not raise if it is true that the dead are not raised" (1 Corinthians 15:14-15). Without the correspondence view of truth, such affirmations carry no meaning.

All this stands in obvious opposition to the current relativist and interfaith view that something can be true for you but not true for me. We'll take this up more fully in chapter 15. But this view would mean that the Christian can say, "Jesus is Lord" and the Muslim that, "Allah is Lord" and all be asked to receive both statements as true because certain sets of believers hold them to be so. Under this view the Church can then comfortably abdicate its missionary and evangelistic responsibility.

But Lewis would insist that if I say, "Jesus is Lord and the final divine revelation to planet earth" and you say, "Allah is God and Muhammad is his ultimate prophet and final revelation", both statements cannot be objectively true because they describe supposed facts or realities which are mutually exclusive. Christians say God has incarnated Himself in Jesus. Muslims say Allah would never incarnate himself. One of these views is true and one is false. In other words, we are refusing to violate the law of noncontradiction, which says that if an affirmation is true, its negation must be false. Says Lewis: "I think we must attack wherever we meet it the nonsensical idea that mutually exclusive propositions about God can both be true."[75]

However, if on the other hand, we make truth dependent upon the group, person or culture holding the belief, anything can become "true". This is manifestly absurd.

For example, we do not allow flat-earthists to teach our children that the earth is flat because we know this to have been falsified by the facts. But if I were a consistent relativist I would have to allow him to teach this to my children because the flat-earthist, for his part, is sincere about it and holds it as true and because I for my part, am not allowed by this relativist to produce an objective basis to make him alter his beliefs by presenting contrary argument, facts or evidence. Such an attitude applied to mathematics, aerodynamics, medicine or science we would consider nonsensical – and dangerous.

After all, who would want to be piloted by a tolerant or broad-minded pilot, unconcerned with the truths of aerodynamics? Or be operated on by a tolerant, broad-minded surgeon unconcerned with the truths of surgery and physiology? Or taught by a tolerant, broad-minded scientist who was relaxed about whether two times two was either four or five and equally relaxed as to whether H_2O or H_3O could be water. Take your pick. Just be sincere. Use whichever formula is meaningful and you can feel good about! Likewise who wants to rest time and eternity on a "take it or leave it" set of relativist options.

No, while we lovingly tolerate people, we do not tolerate what we believe to be error. We believe there are such things as true facts and such things as erroneous facts and the real facts are "unforgiving". "That is the worst of facts," C.S. Lewis once told his father, "they do cramp a fellow's style!" So we must come to terms with them. For example, with regard to the claim that both the incarnation and the resurrection are facts of history, are they or are they not?

"All I am doing," Lewis once said, "is asking people to face the facts and to understand the questions which Christianity claims to answer."

What Lewis believed to be factually true in Christianity

First of all, like fellow author Francis Schaeffer, Lewis believed in "The God who is there", that is, theism. He believed that God created the heavens and earth and humans "in His image". Therefore he rejected "naturalism", which says that all that exists and that we can know consists of the sense-perceptible world. "No," says Lewis, "Jehovah is a real being" and naturalism is thus plain wrong to deny this.

Lewis also believed in a supernatural power of evil called the Devil (his Screwtape). This is "a dark power in the universe – a mighty evil spirit" who is "the power behind death, disease and sin."

By extension therefore, he believed in a realm of evil supernaturalism acting on the human race and which produced a historic space-time "fall of man", causing us to "fall" from the state in which God made us into something else less than fully human. Ever since then, Satan has gained a major foothold on planet earth and we are in "enemy-occupied territory", in consequence of which we are living in a "spiritual civil war".

This was intensified in the incarnation of God in Jesus Christ. And in the New Testament we have this authoritative "story of how the rightful king has landed in disguise and is calling us all to take part in a great campaign of sabotage." This is what the mission of the Church is all about. Lewis was not fussy about theories of the atonement, but he was quite sure that on the Cross where "the sinless man suffers for the sinful" and in the death of Jesus (as by the death of Aslan the Lion, the Jesus symbol in the Narnia stories), the way has been opened both into rational, joyful living here and now and into heaven after death for those who believe. Heaven to him was very real and likewise hell, though on their exact nature or content he would not be overly drawn, except that either God or Satan will eventually say "Mine!" of everything that exists, including every human.

But God, who has provided forgiveness and eternal life through Christ, will never willingly consign anyone to perdition. It will be people's own choice or lack thereof. "The damned are, in one sense", said Lewis, "successful rebels to the end ... the doors of hell are locked on the inside."[76]

Lewis, of course, also believed in miracles as true and wrote a book with that title. Rejecting that "Nature is the whole show"[77], he did not see a miracle as "something which breaks the laws of nature", but rather as an "interference" or "invasion" of the laws of nature and not "a contradiction or outrage" to them. The fact is that if death and resurrection are central to the universal story and its plot, then miracles are not inconsistent with this. "If you have hitherto disbelieved in miracles", he writes, "it is worth pausing a moment to consider whether this is not chiefly because you thought you had discovered what the story was really about – that atoms and time and space and economics and politics were the main plot." If they were, miracles could have no place. But if God and Jesus and the resurrection and the Holy Spirit are the main plot, everything changes. And of course, "the central miracle is the incarnation." All the others fit round it and if it really happened, it is the central historical fact of our planet and the one which gives meaning to all else.

Conclusion

There is much yet to be said of this category of the true and factual in Lewis' thought, but some of that will come in the next chapter.

In the meantime, we reiterate that the Holy Spirit in the believer will press him or her to witness to Jesus Christ, to defend the truth of the Gospel, to uphold the reality of the miraculous, to defend the faith and like C.S. Lewis, to give "a reason [*apologia*] for the hope" (1 Peter 3:15) that is in us.

Chapter Fourteen 14

Witnessing to an Objective Moral Law

We have noted that Christians are called to be witnesses – witnesses to Jesus Christ, witnesses to the truth of the Gospel, witnesses to the authority of the Bible as God's Word. We also witness through seeking to live holy, godly and loving lives in the power of the Holy Spirit.

However, in this day of changing and relativist ethics and morals, it is also vital that we witness to a universal moral law that God has put in His world to guide and control the behaviour of humans. If we do not, we leave the world and ourselves floundering in a sea of moral and intellectual relativism.

At the *Oxbridge '98* conference already spoken about, C.S. Lewis' book, *The Abolition of Man*, was often mentioned, along with one of its chapters entitled "Men Without Chests". Reading this book is not for the fainthearted but it deals with things that are important and relevant to the present time. It tackles the current notion that objective and eternally valid moral truths and standards are up for question.

The book's curious subtitle *"Reflections on education with special reference to the teaching of English in the upper forms of schools"*, springs from the three lectures that Lewis was invited to deliver at Durham University after having reviewed a book by two English teachers. In their book, the authors had set out their views on teaching English and Lewis used the moment to attack the views of certain teachers (in schools, universities and theological colleges) plus other *influencers* of public opinion. The ethics proposed in their book were relative and changeable, since they taught that both aesthetic and moral values are purely subjective and not based on any objective moral law or set of standards. Lewis referred to such a standard as the *Tao*, a Chinese word for *Way* (as we'll see later). Such people, he said, could be called "men without chests".

Men without chests

Who are these strange people? At *Oxbridge '98*, James Packer shed some light on this peculiar title, explaining that it was "a bit of Platonic analysis which comes from Plato's Republic." For Plato, between the mind (located in the head) and the belly is the chest, where lay the spirit or heart, understood as character or formed character. The latter has learned from the mind to direct us habitually along the path which the mind knows to be morally right. Our aim should be to channel our desires along that path, rather than let desire (located in the belly) lead the whole person astray.

Packer further noted that Lewis was accusing contemporary culture of subjectivism and of refusing to acknowledge the universal values which ought to be taught to children from their youth up. This, he said, would produce human beings "without chests", that is with minds adrift and bereft of moral conviction and spiritual wisdom, and operating alongside a whole range of uncontrolled desires.

People without chests will be led by their strongest desires and their minds will be so irrational that they will not even make sense of life. They will, says Lewis have "lost the *Tao*", that is, those morals and values common to all religions and observed in the absolute standards that Christians have claimed to be given to the world in the General Revelation, as seen in the first two chapters of Romans. When this is lost, then so too is the "chest", that is, the whole heritage of developed wisdom. We become cultural castaways, lost in the cosmos, with life becoming merely a matter of "existing" rather than real living. We lose our way, life does not make sense and at such times we need the help of someone who, by the grace of God, will bring us the light of the Gospel so that we may find ourselves.

Lewis was obviously gunning for those who train young minds

to deny or reject objective concepts of morality or value. As Packer saw it, Lewis was intending to "highlight the dreadful effects of the slippage into subjectivism", which he saw going on all around him. Slip into subjectivism and you lose truth and joy. You lose freedom and wisdom as a result of rebellion against the cosmic order. Lewis was challenging the modern "values-free" intellectuals and sceptics whom he saw as people with heads but no hearts, or having hearts without reading them properly. They present values as being in some way "unreal", as compared to "facts", especially those of science. Lewis saw them as being responsible for many ills in society, most notably for reproducing their own kind among the young, a species of learned young experts who are likewise "without chests". Such people, by subordinating the human spirit and mind to the processes of nature (as if there was nothing more to reality than nature), actually bring about the abolition of humanity, since they eradicate that which makes us distinctively human.

Additionally, charges Lewis: "it is an outrage that they should be commonly spoken of as intellectuals. This gives them the chance to say that he who attacks them attacks Intelligence. It is not so. They are not distinguished from other men by any unusual skill in finding truth ... Their heads are no bigger than the ordinary: it is the atrophy of the chest beneath that makes them seem so."[78] What he is doing here is to issue a wake-up call to a generation of people busy supervising their own demise.

Values-free education

The consequence of this is the development of "values-free" education, whether in the teaching of English, or science, or sexuality and morals, etc. Society thus catastrophically and increasingly loses its way. It begins more desperately than ever to need, but not find, leaders and opinion-makers with the very qualities we are being taught to reject. This makes people suddenly begin to cry out for something that will operate as a "liaison officer between cerebral man and visceral man." The search is for "this middle element" by which "man is man". In other words, we are searching for and needing something that makes us uniquely human.[79]

The link between our intellect and the animal part of us – the "middle element" – is the "chest", says Lewis, the heart in which the conscience and value system is located. If that is in place, then qualities of the chest/heart such as honesty, purity, morality, courage, magnanimity and feeling (sentiment) will operate. This is what is needed to save us, but prevailing philosophies are teaching us to reject these qualities as irrelevant or unreal.

Commenting on this, Packer remarked: "How can we wonder now that we have people living in adult bodies with childish and utterly unformed characters who simply become Apostles of irrational, violent behaviour, breaking all bounds and doing so simply because that is the feeling they have at the moment?"

Again from Lewis: "Such is the tragicomedy of our situation, we continue to clamour for those very qualities we are rendering impossible ... In a sort of ghastly simplicity we remove the organ and demand the function. We make men without chests and expect of them virtue and enterprise. We laugh at honour and are shocked to find traitors in our midst. We castrate and bid the geldings be fruitful."[80] In practice, this means that we have people teaching no values to their pupils. Then the teachers are shocked by the shameless, amoral behaviour of their pupils. There are also academics without chests and even ministers of religion without chests.

For Lewis, the latter is the villain of the piece, what he calls the "thoroughly modern, liberal-minded clergyman", or the "over-acculturated cleric" who cannot believe he could land up in hell, "penalised" for his "honest opinions, even assuming, for the sake of argument, that those opinions were mistaken."[81] To be sincere but hopelessly wrong, says Lewis, is perilous to our salvation, perhaps especially if it has caused us to lead others astray! But where did all this relativising and denying of the Gospel begin? What are its origins? To Lewis it begins with teachers without chests, this time in theological colleges. In his book *The Great Divorce*, Lewis' character, Dick, a pastor in heaven, confronts this tragedy with his old friend, just arrived by bus from hell for a visit to the edge of heaven: "Friend, let us be frank. Our opinions were not honestly come by. We simply found ourselves in contact with a certain current of ideas and plunged into it because it seemed modern and successful.

At College, you know, we just started automatically writing the kind of essays that get good marks and saying the kind of things that won applause. When, in our whole lives, did we honestly face, in solitude, the one question on which all turned: whether after all the Supernatural might not in fact occur? When did we put up one moment's real resistance to the loss of our faith? ... We didn't want the other to be true. We were afraid of crude Salvationism, afraid of a breach with the spirit of the age, afraid of ridicule, afraid (above all) of real spiritual fears and hopes ... Having allowed oneself to drift, unresisting, unpraying, accepting every half-conscious solicitation from our desires, we reached a point where we no longer believed the Faith."[82]

The Great Divorce however, is not primarily about intellectual dishonesty, but more about the attempt to blur right and wrong, which nevertheless has its roots in intellectual dishonesty. Notes Lewis: "The attempt is based on the belief that reality never presents us with an absolutely unavoidable 'either-or'; that, granted skill and patience and (above all) time enough, some way of embracing both alternatives (i.e. good and evil) can always be found; that mere development or adjustment or refinement will somehow turn evil into good without our being called on for a final and total rejection of anything we should like to retain. This belief I take to be a disastrous error."[83]

However, all need not be lost if there is repentance and a going back to identify where we went wrong. Writes Lewis: "I do not think that all who choose wrong roads perish; but their rescue consists in being put back on the right road. A wrong sum can be put right: but only by going back till you find the error and working it afresh from that point, never by simply going on. Evil can be undone, but it cannot 'develop' into good ... It is still 'either-or.'"[84] In *The Abolition of Man*, the issue for Lewis is whether we will choose the Tao and the God behind it and see where that leads, or not. Only by facing this can we be mightily helped to get us back on track and be kept there.

The *Tao*, the Law, the Way

For Lewis, as we have seen, the *Tao* is that common set of moral beliefs and values about right and wrong which has been found in all major, stable and responsible religions and cultures ever since civilisation began.

In his appendix to *The Abolition of Man*, Lewis lists many of these values as drawn from Hindu, Confucian, Babylonian, Egyptian, Hebrew, Platonic, Aristotelian and Christian traditions. "What is common to them," says Lewis, "is something we cannot neglect. It is the doctrine of objective value, the belief that certain attitudes are really true, and others really false, to the kind of thing the universe is and the kind of things we are."[85] Within the *Tao*, Lewis would find such notions as basic justice, truthfulness, kind-heartedness, mercy, magnanimity, respect for parents and elders, the wrongness of murder, stealing or lying, the necessity of looking after widows and orphans, the unacceptability of incest and the obligation not to abandon one's wife or children.

Lewis sees this as not one among a series of possible systems of values, but the sole source of all the value judgements there are.

He notes that "if it is rejected, all value is rejected. If any value is retained, it is retained. The effort to refute it and raise a new system of value in its place is self-contradictory. There never has been, and never will be, a radically new judgement of value in the history of the world. What purport to be new systems or (as they now call them) 'ideologies', all consist of fragments from the *Tao* itself, arbitrarily wrenched from their context in the whole and then swollen to madness in their isolation, yet still owing to the *Tao* and to it alone such validity as they possess."[86]

It was this objective value system that was missing in the English textbook sent to Lewis by the two schoolmasters, outlining their approach in teaching English to schoolboys. Their lack of an objective value or truth system, would in Lewis' view de-humanise the schoolboys they taught, by destroying rationality and morality, because it is this *Tao*, this bedrock of basic values, which defines us as humans as distinct from animals. "Stepping out of the *Tao*", says Lewis, "they have stepped into the void. Nor are their subjects necessarily unhappy men. They are not men at all: they are artefacts. Man's final conquest has proved to be the abolition of Man."[87]

Elaborating on this in his book *Mere Christianity*, Lewis also explodes the notion of basic morality and the *Tao* being culturally conditioned, or just a social construct, as when it is claimed that different civilisations have different moralities. "But this is not so," says Lewis. "There have been differences between their moralities, but these have never amounted to anything like a total difference ... I need only ask the reader to think what a totally different morality would mean. Think of a country where people were admired for running away in battle, or where a man felt proud of double-crossing all the people who had been kindest to him. You might just as well try to imagine a country where two and two made five ... Likewise selfishness has never been admired. Men have differed as to whether you should have one wife or four. But they have always agreed that you must not simply have any woman you liked."[88]

In the Old Testament, this Law, this moral code written into the fabric of reality, is expressed in the Ten Commandments. For the New Testament, "The Way" (Acts 16:17; 18:26; 2 Peter 2:15; 2 Peter 2:21) as personalised in Jesus is not only the Way to salvation, but the Way for everything: for living, loving, behaving and doing. To follow "The Way" is to live out and co-operate with the moral law (*Tao*) written into the fabric of the universe by Jesus Himself, the Creator of everything, for "without Him was not anything made that was made" (John 1:3). For Paul in Romans 2:15a, the *Tao* is discerned, I believe, in what he calls "the law written on their hearts" and to which our "conscience" bears "witness" (2:15b). And it is this, of course, along with God's testimony to Himself in the created order ("the things that are made") which leaves us "without excuse" (Romans 1:20) before the just demands or judgements of a holy God. And being "without excuse" and guilty before God, we now have to face something awesome, namely that we are in a terrible fix.

The terrible fix we are in

We are guilty before a holy God, the one who is the Giver of this Law, which puts us in a terrible fix. Without even opening our Bibles we are aware of two realities, observes Lewis: "First that human beings, all over the earth, have this curious idea that they ought to behave in a certain way, and cannot really get rid of it. Secondly, that they do not, in fact, behave in that way. They know the Law of Nature; they break it. These two facts are the foundation of all clear thinking about ourselves and the universe we live in."[89] At this point, as Roman Catholic scholar Richard John Neuhaus noted at *Oxbridge '98*, Lewis might well ask, as he often did, "is it not true? Do you not find it to be so?"

Conclusion

In concluding this chapter, where we have again let C.S. Lewis be our teacher, we have to say, "Yes, we find it to be so." Yes, we find that there is such a thing as a moral code written into the fabric of the universe and into our hearts (chests) and into nature by God Himself. And we find it to be so that there is such a thing as right and wrong. And we find it to be so that this moral law is known and discerned in natural revelation by the major religions of the world, by the dictates of conscience and by the constituted order of things in nature. Hence, in passing, we note that Paul's condemnation in Romans 2 of homosexual sins is that they are "against Nature" – that is, against the constituted natural and moral order of creation –against the *Tao*, in fact.

All of this being so, "we have cause to be uneasy", because faced with this Law (*Tao*) of God, and with absolute goodness and its demands, we see "all have sinned and fall short of the glory of God" (Romans 3:23). That's why we are in "a terrible fix". And that's how we become ready for the Gospel and for what Jesus has done for us in His atoning death upon the Cross.

Once we understand that we are in "a terrible fix", Christianity begins to talk to us. And it tells us the good news that this "law was our custodian until Christ came, that we might be justified by faith" (Galatians 3:24). It tells us that we are sinners in need of a Saviour. And knowing all this, we are now ready to hear about Jesus and the cross, and forgiveness and eternal life and heaven for all who believe. And as we respond to this and follow it, there is also the prospect of built-up chests for all of us! Talk about amazing grace!

However, we have a problem! Why? Because the kind of line taken in this chapter in terms of Christian witness is one which contradicts the spirit of the age and the contemporary embrace of religious pluralism, interfaith and the supremacy of an all-embracing tolerance! Let's think more about this!

15 Chapter Fifteen

Tolerance, Truth and Religious Pluralism

The Bible, as we have seen, and the moral law as we have looked at it, require a clear, unequivocal affirmation of biblical truth and an unapologetic embrace of biblical ethics.

But this cuts across the moral and intellectual climate of the times where both intellectual truth and moral principle are viewed in highly relativistic terms.

So this species of relativism is definitely one of the new hot potato issues facing the contemporary Church. It basically focuses in on other religions and their truth claims and how Christians are to respond to these in our religiously pluralistic society.

Let's say right up front that there are some very proper challenges relating to Christian tolerance. But a widespread not-so-proper belief is developing that all truths are relative. This needs questioning. The view says: "You have your opinion, I have mine. You like Jesus, I like Buddha. He likes crystal balls and she is into Eastern mysticism. So what? Surely sincerity is all that matters and all roads lead to God anyway. Are we not all worshiping the same God? Are not all ways to God equally valid?"

Well, I'm not so sure. But we must tread carefully for this is a real minefield indeed. What then can we say?

New place

I acknowledge that we are in a new place in terms of the very self-conscious religious pluralism developing in our world everywhere today and especially in my own country of South Africa. I have no problem with this. It is both right and inevitable. I am also comfortable with the playing field being levelled by the absence of any special privileges for Christians.

So how then are we to respond to people of other living faiths? I believe we should begin first of all with repentance and contrition for the arrogant and dismissive manner in which we Christians have often in our past record handled people of other faiths. We have not always had grounds for pride. Our approach needs to be humble and sensitive so that other people's convictions are respected. There should also be an open-mindedness and a willingness to learn and understand.

An obligation to proclaim Christ

So, while one may listen sensitively in order to understand, I don't believe Christians should ever surrender the obligation to call people, whoever they are or whatever they believe, to faith in Christ. Our Lord told us to go into all the world and proclaim the Gospel *to every person*, calling each one to come in repentance and faith to the Living Christ who is Saviour, Lord and God. Remember, Christianity began in the context of another living faith, namely Judaism, and the Apostle Paul found no problem in saying that the Gospel was "for the Jew first and then for the Greek" (Romans 1:16).

Tolerance

Let's register first of all that there are, as John Stott has observed, various kinds of tolerance.[90]

Legal tolerance. The first is what has been called legal tolerance, which requires that everybody's religious rights, including minority religious rights, should be adequately protected by law. Christians should demand this. Constitutions should protect it.

Social tolerance. Then there is social tolerance, which requires respect for all people, whatever their views, so that we appreciate their position and do nothing to jeopardise the spirit of good neighbourliness. Christians should also promote this in a genuine spirit of love.

It is not easy, but clearly obligatory. How much we fail in this!

Intellectual tolerance. There is also intellectual tolerance, which requires a fine balancing act from Christians. On the one hand we have to respect people's intellectual views. But on the other hand we can cultivate a mind so broad that it accommodates every opinion, even if it is false or evil, without ever detecting anything to reject or question. This is not a virtue. It is, in many ways, feeble-mindedness. Christians who stand on the view that truth and goodness are finally revealed in Jesus Christ cannot possibly adopt this posture. In fact, this conviction, as part of historical Christianity, was articulated by William Temple, when Archbishop of Canterbury, once said, "Christianity is, I am persuaded, a profoundly intolerant religion."

Again we must stress that this is not the intolerance of other people, but the intolerance of error, in the same way that the mathematician will not tolerate someone seriously maintaining that 2 x 2 = 5. People's freedom of belief does not make their ideas the same as, or equal to, a proper scientific view of the world. And to disagree with someone is not intolerance, but part of the struggle for intellectual integrity concerning the data of life.

David Hewetson of Australia has written perceptively of this, saying: "As I see it tolerance in religion has only one role: it is there to *preserve the rights of all men everywhere to believe what they choose to believe.* The trouble is that in this tolerant age many people do not understand this. They have put tolerance on such a prominent pedestal that it is often accorded the right to do much more than protect human rights; indeed to do things for which it is not designed. In particular men make it the judge of whether things are true or false."[91]

Hewetson adds: "Tolerance (rightly) declares that all men are free to believe what they choose to believe. But many people assume (incorrectly and illogically) that this makes all beliefs equally correct, or at least above criticism. Now let me *illustrate*: A man is free to believe that the world is flat (and some men do). If he is persecuted for it tolerance demands that we do all in our power to protect him. But his freedom of belief does not make his ideas the same as, or equal to, a proper scientific view of the world. And to disagree with him is not intolerance, but just plain common sense. So tolerance cannot decide what is right or wrong, true or false, and we should not ask it to. It already has a most valuable, indeed essential, role. It preserves our right to an opinion no matter how mistaken others may think us. And it allows us to be tolerant of other people's beliefs without necessarily agreeing with them."[92]

Basically we are preserving everyone's freedom of opinion without declaring all those opinions to be correct or true.

Revelation

That said, we have to ask ourselves whether there is a total discontinuity between Christianity and other religions. Are we affirming that all truth is contained in Christianity and no truth in the others? The answer is obviously, "No". On the basis of what is often called *general revelation* in nature, in the universe and in ourselves, all human beings are able to understand volumes of truth. Paul, in Romans 1 and 2, says that from the creation of both the world and human beings, we can discern the invisible nature of God and His eternal power and deity, these things being "clearly perceived in the things that have been made." This being so, people are "without excuse" (Romans 1:20). Everyone can discern these truths through *general revelation* as revealed in creation, but there is also further *general revelation* in conscience as Paul explains in his epistles, especially in Romans 2:15. All the great religious leaders of the world had and have access to this *general revelation*. And much of this truth, along with its ethical implications, is contained in other religions. However, in Christian belief, such truths about the nature of God and reality as have in other religions been correctly deduced from general revelation should produce a readiness to receive God's *special revelation* in Christ and in the Judaeo-Christian Scriptures.

In the Gifford Lectures, (whose parameters required that nobody step into *special revelation*), Archbishop William Temple set forth his brilliant thesis in *Nature, Man and God*, that *natural revelation* leaves all the world on tiptoe "and in a hunger" waiting for the *special revelation* of God in Christ.[93]

So everything that is true in other religions is a preparation for the Gospel. So although we are open to people of other faiths and tolerant of their different beliefs, we nevertheless avoid the openness of indifference to truth – truth being coherence with the facts as they are – but embrace the openness that invites everyone into the quest for knowledge and certitude in Christ.

In this way we differ from the people who prefer the twilight of free thought to what C.S. Lewis once called "the tyrannous noon of revelation."

Law of antithesis

Another corollary of this is that we can never accept the view – like the Queen judging the race in *Alice in Wonderland* – that "everyone has won." The law of antithesis, we reiterate, says that A is not non-A and that two contradictory statements cannot both be true at the same time. Because the major religions of the world are not saying the same things, except possibly in certain ethical arenas, there must be within the dialogue the question of truth and error, especially when, far from agreeing, they contradict each other, often at very central and cardinal points of teaching.

To quote David Hewetson again: "Do world religions actually agree with each other? In some things, yes. But in many basic issues, not at all. The briefest examination of their major claims shows no possible hope of amalgamation. For example, how could you combine Hinduism's plural and impersonal gods represented by images, with Judaism or Islam's conviction that God is one and personal and that he must not be visibly depicted? How could the agnosticism of classical Buddhism join up with Christianity and Islam's fervent belief in God's existence? Or how could you merge Islam's rejection of the divinity, crucifixion and resurrection of Jesus with Christianity's conviction that this is the heart and centre of everything?"[94]

Likewise, the leading devotees of world religions would not say that sincerity and devotion are all that matter. No Buddhist would accept that deliverance from the illusions of selfhood was an inconsequential conviction. Nor would any Muslim feel that the unity of God can be compromised on in any way. And a Christian who does not believe in the deity, atoning death and resurrection of Jesus Christ cannot merit the name Christian. So, despite the relativism which today we call tolerance, these things cannot be ignored. The differences are there and they are very real. Hard thinking must be done about the truth or otherwise of the very different truth claims in the various religions of the world. In the long run, major choices have to be made relating to what is true and what is not. This should not and need not violate anywhere the laws of love, tolerance and mutual respect.

Co-operation

Finally, where and when should Christians co-operate with people of other faiths? I believe that in all matters of common humanity, issues of justice, environmental protection, hunger and poverty – in other words, everything relating to our doctrine of creation, humankind and personhood – there should be co-operation between Christians and people of other faiths or no faith at all. Therefore, if the interfaith movement, for example, calls for co-operation in those areas, I for one have no problem. But if co-operation concerns missiology, soteriology (i.e. issues of salvation) or related matters, I would find very serious difficulties. And I don't honestly think these are rooted in ignorance or arrogance but in an orthodox theological understanding of the truth that is in Jesus and the Judaeo- Christian Scriptures.

To avoid this issue, in my view, requires trying to get around Jesus altogether. And was not He the one who said: "I am the Way, the Truth and the Life; no one comes to the Father but by me" (John 14:6)? Beyond that, He prayed: "Sanctify them in the Truth; Thy Word is Truth" (John 17:17). Such a prayer, however, is pretty much anathema in a contemporary culture which calls itself "Postmodern". This being the case, we need in the home-straight of this volume to go deeper into the cultural context of Postmodernism and ask how we got here and how, once here, we cope as Christians with the intellectual and cultural environment in which we now find ourselves.

16 Chapter Sixteen

A Background to Postmodernism

Our world seems to be at a very strange place, a place we have never been in before. Nothing seems to be sure. Nothing is steady. Old foundations and values seem to have gone and new ones are too untested and untried to have taken root. Wherever we stand appears to be on shifting sand and we shift with it. In many ways we seem to be living between two worlds. One world is past and with a culture dead or dying and the other refusing as yet to be born. We are in-between people, neither here nor there – in reality, nowhere and adrift. Indeed the period we have been destined to live in seems to be one of parenthesis. We are in "brackets", curiously cut off from the past, but not knowing how to access the future.

A time of shattering cultural upheaval

Part of the problem appears to lie in the fact that we are not only *Postmodern*, to use a common phrase whose meaning we will explore shortly, but *post-everything*. It is a time of shattering cultural upheaval.

For example, we seem to be *post-moral*, because the current notion of behaviour seems to be that anything goes: "You do your thing, I'll do mine. Let him do his and she hers, and let's not judge one another or anyone."

Then in a funny paradoxical sort of a way we are *post-God* and *post-spiritual*, while also being pro-God and pro-spiritual at one and the same time. The fact is that our culture at one level is thoroughly pagan, totally atheistic, secular, God-rejecting, immoral, amoral, proud, arrogant, autonomous, non-spiritual and individualistic. We say along with the poet W.E. Henley: "I am the master of my fate, I am the captain of my soul."

But then no sooner have we affirmed that we are post-God and able to run our lives as full-blown secularists, than suddenly we find that we are not only pagan but *post-pagan*, because paradoxically, deep down and in apparent inner contradiction, our world now finds itself hankering after some species of spirituality, almost *any* spirituality, and searching for some sort of god or any god or all gods. We act individualistically, but we long for community and connectedness. We build our lives round materialism but we are *post-materialist* because we are sick of materialism and realise it can do nothing for the inner person. We affirm that we are *post-sin*, but in reality we find that doing all those things that were previously called sinful, actually does deep-level damage to our inner beings and robs us of what we used to call happiness.

On the sexual and behavioural front, we act as if we are *post-marriage*, and yet deep down we are almost *post-post-marriage*, because people everywhere long to have deep and steady male/female relationships, with family life and care and security for children working properly and satisfactorily.

Likewise we are *post-functionalism*, because as an age we behave in a way that is endlessly dysfunctional. But the consequences of that make us want *post-dysfunctionalism*, because we discover that we are longing for things to function properly and we will go to endless seminars and read countless books on how to make our homes, work experience or inner psychological mechanisms more functional and congenial.

Paradox

There is another paradox. We bow, worship and prostrate ourselves at the shrine of technology but part of us is *post-technology* too, because we have an inner sense that technology has got out of hand and has the potential to lead us profoundly astray. So there is a paradoxical yearning to get away from it all, to get back to the simple life, to re-embrace nature, to get into the bush or to the forests and look at birds and animals. And when we do, part of the deal is that there must be no cell-phones, computers or e-mail facilities anywhere in sight! In fact, we enjoy more those times when we sit around campfires and operate by candlelight or hurricane lamps rather than electricity. Come to think of it, while we are *post-the-ox-wagon* and its pace, we are perhaps beginning to hanker for the *post-speed* age, as we call on ourselves to slow down, find more leisure time, move at a more leisured pace, to discover "margin" in our lives. So while part of us is addicted to frenzy and the adrenalin rush that goes with it, another part of us knows that frenzy ultimately is an enemy of the soul and the space-age pace of life is something we warn our children against.

American author Mary Pipher captures another aspect of this period of paradox in her book, *The Shelter of Each Other*. "In the 1930s we had an enormous economic crisis. Today we have the poverty of consumerism, which means never having enough. We are impoverished in a different way – we are, to quote Peter Rowan, 'Thirsty in the rain'. Many of us do work that we neither feel proud of nor enjoy. We are too rushed to do the things we really value. Ironies abound. With more entertainment we are more bored. With more sexual information and stimulation, we experience less sexual pleasure. In a culture focussed on feelings, people grow emotionally numb. With more time saving devices, we have less time. With more books, we have fewer readers. With more mental health professionals, we have worse mental health. Today we are in a more elusive crisis, a crisis of meaning with emotional, spiritual and social aspects. We hunger for values, community and something greater than ourselves to dedicate our lives to. We wake in the night sorry for ourselves and our planet."[95]

In the modern Church too we have moved into the period of *post-denominationalism*, where denominations mean very little and people worship and move between denominations with both rapidity and fluidity, or even have a worship style that embraces several different denominations at once!

Of course, we have our Bibles and although we are thankful that the Bible is the world's bestseller, at another level it is the world's least read bestseller. We love to have it on our shelves and even dip into it now and then, but our reluctance to apply it thoroughly, so that our lifestyles are changed, is perilously manifest. We have Christianity everywhere, but it seems to affect little the cultures in which it seems to thrive most. We want to be *post-Bible* and *post-Christianity*, but part of us longs for the spiritual food and meaning that come from the Bible and from Christianity.

Yes, it is a time of paradox. A time of *post-everythingism*. In fact, we are probably living in one of the most shattering and disorienting cultural upheavals since the fall of the Roman Empire.

How did we get here?

In order for us to cope with this time of parenthesis in which we are living, it is essential in my view, to try to fathom how we got here so that we can figure out a bit more clearly how to move on from where we are, to where we would like to be. And perhaps the place where we need to go looking for clues is in the arena of so-called Modernity and Postmodernity.

Many people say that the period of so-called Modernity ran for the 200-year period from approximately 1790 to 1990. It was a time of emphasis on the autonomy of man and of human reason. But many found this curiously inadequate and it began to give way to a period of so-called Postmodernity, where a new set of ground rules for our thinking processes began to develop.

But maybe before looking at either Modernity or Postmodernity, we need to try to get an overview of what happened before that. So let us go back a bit and pick up some headlines in the sweep of history to see where we fit.

The Graeco-Roman world

Our Gospel and Christian faith, of course, began and found its root in what we now speak of as the Graeco-Roman world. It was a world that spanned pretty much the first 350 years of this AD era. It was a world in which there were many gods who had to be kept satisfied and placated when human beings got it wrong. The Roman Emperor began to be perceived as embodying or representing this plurality of divine beings. He accordingly had to be worshipped and death was the consequence for refusing to do so. It was also a world of culture, literature, art and brilliant writing. The Roman and Greek games were important and there was a strong exaltation of the physical body as housing a vitally active mind. This way exhibited the principle of "the sound mind in a sound body."

Into this world, around AD30 came Christianity arising out of the public and earthly ministry of our Lord Jesus Christ. In the years that followed His crucifixion and resurrection, Christians brought an astonishing witness in which they outlived, outloved and outdied their adversaries and competitors.

Finally, when the Emperor Constantine was converted in AD311 and issued an edict of tolerance jointly with the Eastern Emperor Licinius at Milan in AD313, the victory of Christians was signalled and sealed. The Cross was put on Roman coins stamped with the insignia: *"In hoc signo vincis"* ("In this sign you will conquer"). Christianity was now the official religion of the Roman Empire and the era of Christendom was born.

The era of Christendom

Now follows one of the most extraordinary periods in all of human history. For some 1,400 years, in spite of some wretchedly bad behaviour from leaders in the Church and much awful corruption and worldliness, a worldview held sway across most of Europe in which God was at the centre and Jesus was there as the Lord of the Universe and Cosmos. Indeed, Christian theology became "the queen of the sciences" and all other disciplines found their central point of reference in the Person of Christ, the Bible and Christian theology. Jesus became the key to interpreting not just religious and spiritual life, but all life.

Especially important and central to this worldview was the notion of regularity in the Universe. In other words, the Universe was seen as regular because it is based upon and created by a God who operates rationally and according to laws that He has established and which give life a certain predictability. The sun rises and sets, the seasons come and go, the law of gravity and other physical laws operate because they are grounded in the mind and will of a reasonable, rational God. This principle of regularity became the way by which an explosion of learning and science could take place. Scholars found that by using their reason under God, and by believing that there was such a thing as truth, laws could be uncovered and discovered and certain universal principles could begin to be articulated and laws formulated.

There were also universal moral laws to be obeyed and certain things were seen as right and others as wrong, as good or evil, as beautiful or ugly, as beneficial or harmful. This was a world in which the Church ruled and exercised a strong authority. What the Church said was the way things were. It meant that all of life was interpreted by God, the Bible and the Church and could not be challenged. Most particularly, the story of Jesus provided the inner clue as to how all of life was to be understood and interpreted.

Christian theologians taught that there were basically two books of revelation by which humankind could gain an understanding of God and of the reality in which they lived. The first was what they called *Natural Revelation*, or "the book of nature" where certain truths about God could be gleaned by observation and reason. Secondly there was *Special Revelation*, which was found in the Bible as a disclosure of God and reality that could not come naturally and by nature, but had to come supernaturally and through the Spirit of God.

And in all of this the Christian Church was the basic teaching authority, informing people how things were, how people should behave, and pretty much what they had to think.

The late David Bosch, the South African missiologist, wrote that from Augustine through to Luther: "The individual was never emancipated and autonomous but was regarded, first and foremost, as standing in a relationship to God and the Church."[96]

Of course this extraordinary and effectively unchallenged authority of the Church was fine and wonderful while it was getting things right. But what would be the consequences if it began to get anything wrong? This is what occurred with the arrival into that world of Galileo Galilei (1564-1642). Until then the Church had taught with conviction and authority that the sun and the planets revolved around the earth. But this upstart scientist, this heretic, this misguided intellectual, now said that the latter view was wrong: the earth and the planets revolve around the sun. And he was right! Suddenly the Church's authority and dogmatism took a tremendous pounding and Science and Reason began to become more consequential and authoritative. Suddenly the teaching voice of the Church was no longer seen as ultimate, final or infallible. Science had shown itself superior, and in demonstrating that, a new age was born. This age came to be known as The Age of Reason or The Enlightenment and ran through much of the 1700s.

The Enlightenment period

At first the two books of God's revelation to humans, namely Nature and Revelation, were not seen as standing in contradiction or in competition. Science was still meant to be the handmaiden of theology and theology was still the Queen of the Sciences. Yet it could not be denied that the seeds of a new movement were being planted in the intellectual and spiritual soil of Europe. Through them, Reason would slowly be elevated to a place of supremacy over so-called Revelation and the teaching authority of the Church. In a sense what was happening was a gradual movement of placing humankind, rather than God, at the centre of reality. Suddenly the theologian was no longer the final authority and was replaced by the scientist. Nature slowly became more important than revelation and grace. As this happened, human beings were seen to be more and more autonomous, more and more free agents, more and more able to call the shots and more and more able to explain things without the help of God, the Bible or theology.

We should not think in all of this that God was totally removed from the scene, but He was no longer centre-stage as in previous times.

To come back again to my late friend David Bosch and his affirmation that the Enlightenment frame of mind spanned seven cardinal convictions: "First, its emphasis on reason suggested that the human mind was the indubitable point of departure for all knowing. Second, it divided all of reality into thinking *subjects* and, over against these, *objects* that could be analysed and exploited. Third, it dropped all references to purpose and viewed every process only in terms of cause and effect. Fourth, it put a high premium on progress, on expansion, advance and modernisation. Fifth, it proceeded from the assumption that all true knowledge was factual, value free and neutral. Over against facts there were values, which were not objectively true, the holding of which was, therefore, a matter of taste. Religion was, in the course of time, relegated to this category. Sixth, the Enlightenment proceeded from the assumption that all problems were in principle solvable. Last, it regarded people as emancipated, autonomous individuals, no longer under the tutelage of 'superiors'."[97]

Elsewhere Bosch notes: "A central creed of the Enlightenment, therefore, was faith in humankind. Its progress was assured by the free competition of individuals pursuing their happiness. The free and 'natural' human being was infinitely perfectible and should be allowed to evolve along the lines of his or her own choice. From the earliest beginnings of liberal thought, then, there was a tendency in the direction of indiscriminate freedom. The insatiable appetite for freedom to live as one pleases developed into a virtually inviolable right in the Western 'democracies'. The self-sufficiency of the individual over social responsibilities was exalted to a sacred creed. The corollary of this view was that each individual should also allow all other individuals to think and act as they please. According to this philosophy, the true believer is the real danger."[98]

Any exclusivist or extravagant claims for Jesus Christ or Christianity were thus radically relativised. Although Bosch sees it "as an over-simplification to juxtapose Enlightenment and Christian faith as if they must be implacable foes, nevertheless the hard fact was that a process of secularisation was being set in motion which would lead in time to a profound entrance into secular society. This process would give birth to what many have called the 'phenomenon of modernity.'"[99]

The phenomenon of Modernity

So we now reach the period called Modernism (1790-1990). For many scholars this includes the Enlightenment and post-Enlightenment period. Its roots, as we have indicated, although in the 18th century Enlightenment, gripped the intellectual soul of Europe in many ways from that time until now, in spite of a powerful movement of reaction called Postmodernism which we will look at in a moment. Modernism's basic posture was one of reaction against authority. At various levels it was a flight from authority and particularly the authority of the Church. Modernism wanted liberation from everything to do with the past and the way it had historically laid down the law as to how people should think and behave. With Reason becoming king, the traditional authorities of Jesus Christ and the Bible, especially as these came from the past, were now held suspect. Humankind could now take control and do as they saw fit. German philosophers such as Friedrich Nietzsche (1844-1900) affirmed that human beings could take control over what was around them and overpower it. Humankind was now fully at the centre and in charge.

Writes scholar James Hunter: "Modernity posits an understanding and ordering of the world through an autonomous and human rationality. This plays out at two levels. At a philosophical level, rationality assumes the only reality to be that which can be appropriated empirically by the senses. This reality can be explained logically and scientifically in an ordered system of rationally-derived propositions. Such an assumption slams the door on the very idea of transcendence/supernatural. The world of Nature, of which humanity is a part, is all there is. It is the task of the sciences to explain this world.

"Explanation, however, is not enough. It is essential to achieve mastery over the world through the practical application of rational controls on all aspects of everyday life, in our solving of the great human dilemmas, in our ordering of social relationships in organisations, in our rational management of everything from the day's activities to the next ten years of a career."[100]

However, the horrific reality was that the supposed "Human

Mastery of the World", plus the vast and extraordinary advances in science, technology and medicine did not usher in utopia. In fact, the final outcome of Modernity was a dramatic demonstration of the flawed and sinful nature of human beings without this God whom they had sidelined.

Thus it was that many who had bowed their knees at the shrine of Modernity began to look around with a critical eye at its consequences. They saw two World Wars, the Holocaust killing chambers of Auschwitz and Belsen, plus the Russian Gulags under Stalin in which millions died. Then on all sides there was seen to be rampant despair, moral weightlessness, profound human anxiety, a deep sense of centrelessness and meaninglessness, plus a relational and sexual revolution that had reduced much of life to a psychological and emotional shambles.

Autonomous human reason had certainly proved itself to be intellectually brilliant, but it had brought the world to the very edge of the abyss at all sorts of levels. In a sense it revealed Modernity as exhausted and bankrupt. A reaction was on the way and disillusionment in the air. The godlessness and barrenness of rationalism and intellectualism and all it brought with it began to produce a profound questioning. Surely there must be something more? Surely there must be something spiritual, or transcendent, or godlike, some Superior Force? Later on and in our own times, when the *Star Wars* movies spoke about "the Force", as a power out there able to affect human beings, contemporary young people in their millions flocked to see the films, affirm their central thesis and buy into their notions. Postmodernism was in the process of being born.

17 Chapter Seventeen

Postmodernism and Post-Everythingism

At one level Postmodernism has involved a partial continuation of Modernism, because we still live in an age that exalts the intellect to an extraordinary degree, and which in practical life, still leaves humans at the centre. Nevertheless there is also a reaction to Modernism and an attempt to transcend it. There is a desire to move beyond what Modernism was all about, but we are not quite sure how to do it.

We need to acknowledge that this term "Postmodernism" is a slippery and difficult one, much bandied about. It is not always easy to get a clear and thorough handle on what it means or on its key ideas. And, how Christians and the Church should respond to it is by no means clear. In some ways "Postmodernism" is a code word for some of the tremendous changes and upheaval taking place in Western society.

Alister McGrath says that one of the key causes in the rise of Postmodernism is "the collapse of the confidence in reason, and a more general disillusionment with the so-called 'modern' world. Postmodernism is the intellectual movement which proclaims that the Enlightenment rested on fraudulent intellectual foundations (such as the belief in the omnicompetence of human reason)."[101]

Os Guinness, an insightful Christian cultural analyst, has noted: "Where Modernism was a manifesto of human self-confidence and self-congratulation, Postmodernism is a confession of modesty, if not despair. There is no truth; only truths. There is no grand reason; only reasons. There is no privileged civilisation (or culture, belief, norm and style); only a multiplicity of cultures, beliefs, norms and styles. There is no universal justice; only interests and the competition of interest groups. There is no grand narrative of human progress; only countless stories of where people and their cultures are now. There is no simple reality or any grand objectivity of universal, detached knowledge; only a ceaseless representation of everything in terms of everything else."[102]

It is this sort of intellectual and philosophical reality which gives us in these times the sense I referred to earlier in these pages of standing perennially on shifting sand. Nothing, by these intellectual ground rules, remains stable or sure. All is unsettled. Former foundations are either cracking or already gone in a cultural shift of huge dimensions. Once when I was in Canada I had the privilege of spending time with the late Stanley Grenz, professor of theology and ethics at Regent College in Vancouver, Canada. In his book, *A Primer on Postmodernism*, he says: "The Postmodern consciousness has abandoned the Enlightenment belief in inevitable progress. Postmoderns have not sustained the optimism that characterises previous generations. To the contrary, they evidence a gnawing pessimism. For the first time in recent history, the emerging generation does not share the conviction of their parents that the world is becoming a better place in which to live."[103]

In other words the utopian optimism of most of the 19th and 20th centuries has gone and is being replaced by a species of apocalyptic pessimism.

But most significantly, as Grenz noted, there is something additional here, namely that the dark pessimism of the Postmodern consciousness "operates with a view of truth different from what previous generations espoused ... The modern understanding linked truth with rationality and made reason and logical argumentation the sole arbiters of right belief."[104]

Grenz went on to observe that: "Postmoderns question the concept of universal truth as discovered and proved through rational endeavors. They are unwilling to allow the human intellect to serve as a sole determiner of what we should believe. Postmoderns look beyond reason to nonrational ways of knowing, conferring heightened status on the emotions and intuition."[105]

Truth thus becomes something very unsure and uncertain. In fact, even the notion of truth begins to vanish as Postmoderns see truth as that which basically is located within the individual communities in which we were raised and conditioned. So they reject the Enlightenment search after universal, supra-cultural and timeless truth. Rather do they see truth as that which is simply the expression of how a specific community sees things. In this understanding, truth consists in a number of ground rules that makes personal well-being operative and evident in any given community. So truth is no longer universal but rather local in nature. There is not one truth, but many different truths. This plurality of truths can exist alongside one another and in juxtaposition to each other and even in contradiction to each other. This introduces a species of radical relativism and pluralism.

This is well captured in an entertaining tale John Stott tells of a social worker in Nigeria who once visited a youth in one of the back streets of Lagos. Says Stott: "On his bedside table he found the following books: The Bible, the *Book of Common Prayer*, the Qur'an, three copies of *The Watchtower* (the magazine of the Jehovah's Witnesses), a biography of Karl Marx, a book of Yoga exercises, and what the fellow evidently needed most – a popular paperback entitled *How to Stop Worrying!*"[106]

One British writer, Lynne Franks, has written about her quest: "In June 1992 I started a four-year journey to search for the truth. I found that there are many self-proclaimed prophets and I realise that much discrimination needs to go into the selection of your spiritual path ... I am just a woman on her journey to her truth."[107] It is not a case of her journey to *the* truth, but her journey to *her* truth!

There is no notion of there being any objective truth out there, only a subjective embracing of a personal posture. In a popular magazine article entitled "I Believe in Pik 'n Mix Spirituality", Jane Turney writes: "I am one of a growing number of people who feel we can no longer rely on external authority to run our lives safely – we feel let down by orthodox religions, scientists, politicians, doctors and economists, and think that we have to look for our own answers. This may mean that I visit an astrologer, a Buddhist meditation teacher, and a Christian mystic as part of my search. I do not necessarily mean that I am looking for a quick fix, rather that I recognise that there are many roads to God and that ultimately I am the only person responsible for my journey home."[108]

Tolerance the ultimate virtue

All of this means that tolerance becomes the ultimate virtue in Postmodern thinking and intolerance the ultimate sin. In a world of endless choices and multiple options, we have to place top priority on tolerating those who choose or opt differently from us. Of course it all sounds very sensible, loving, appealing and proper, and would seem to be just the loving way to go. Any other way sounds arrogant, superior and presumptuous. Surely it is more gracious, even godly, to say that truth is what you find for yourself and not what somebody else imposes on you. So I say: "I have something here for you and I ask you to try this for size." I don't say to you "This is the truth, and I urge you to receive and embrace it." That is not permissible. No, one must be polite, Postmodern and totally tolerant. The line is that you have your opinion, I have mine; other people have theirs and all opinions are equally valid. We cannot say, "I am right and you are wrong." In fact, Postmoderns assert that our various belief systems are ultimately the product of the social, community or group context in which we live and they are constructs taken from there. In consequence, what is right for one group is not necessarily right for the other. And what is right in one context may not be right or preferable in another one. So all becomes relative in both the religious and the moral sphere.

But, curiously and paradoxically in other spheres, as we noted in chapter 15 on truth and tolerance, we do still want to hold to the notion of absolutes and truth when it comes to science, mathematics or aerodynamics. So we are happy with scientific or mathematical dogmatism, but not spiritual, religious or theological dogmatism.

But the Christian affirms that if Jesus is indeed Lord of the universe, then His truth, as a description of what is really there and which describes things as they are, permeates everything in the physical, social, moral and spiritual universe.

In the Christian view, as C.S. Lewis reminded us, this means that some things are indeed true and some are not. Some statements cohere with things as they really are, while others do not. Truth is seen as coherence with the facts. It also means that two contradictory statements cannot both be true at the same time. So the Christian says that Jesus Christ died on the Cross and rose again from the dead and that what He did in His death and resurrection is vital for our salvation. Islam on the other hand says that Jesus Christ did not die on the Cross and did not rise again and that salvation is basically by works and not through the grace and mercy of a free gift of forgiveness on the basis of Calvary. We must reaffirm that these two statements and understandings cannot both be true at the same time. Either Jesus did die on the Cross and rise again, or He did not. We cannot say both statements are true.

In other words, we insist again on the validity and importance of the law of antithesis, which says that A is not non-A and that two contradictory statements cannot both be true at the same time.

This means that the Biblical Christian has to reject the line taken by Postmodernism that there exist as many truths as there are communities or individuals within them.

Summing up the postures, tendencies and mind-sets of Postmodernism

In wrapping up here and in drawing from the insights of Grenz, McGrath and others, I believe we can summarise the postures of Postmodernism in the following terms:

- Recognition of religious pluralism in the world. With this the Christian is in agreement.
- A renunciation of intellectual hopes for completeness and certainty because all is tentative. All presumption is therefore gone and all power-plays by which anyone is pressed to believe anything are seen as totally unacceptable.
- A focus on the way societies use language to construct and de-

scribe their own realities, experiences and convictions.
- A preference for the local and specific over against the universal and the abstract.
- Strong doubt that any professed human truth is a simple objective representation of reality and an acceptance that various and differing views cannot be objectively measured in any final sense.
- A renewed interest in narrative and storytelling. This is something which Christians can relate to and use creatively.
- Pessimism and often despair about human progress, the progress notion having been built on the foundations of human reason, scientific technology, materialism and humanistic efforts. The Bible is also pessimistic about human progress in a general sense, but insists that individuals can make huge quantum leaps morally and be transformed spiritually.
- Completely scepticism about any kind of firm or fixed ideology. Rather, it embraces a radical relativism that has no fixed points, absolutes or givens. Truth is simply defined by each individual and community as per its own insights and experiences.
- An insistance that fixed beliefs are naive, as are firm commitments. Beyond that, all authorities, such as the Bible or the Church, are seen as basically misleading, if not corrupt.
- A belief that there is no final or single meaning inherent in any particular literary text, but that the meaning only really emerges as the interpreter enters into different sorts of dialogue with the text. Thus the text is unravelled, or to use their word, "deconstructed". So there are as many different sorts of meanings to a text as there are readers or readings.
- Morals become totally relativised. One can't say one thing is right and another is wrong. Everything is a matter of "pick 'n mix", do your own thing, chart your own course. In other words, go with the culture, follow the morals or inclinations of the moment, and let the 21st century secular community decide how you behave and think.

All this leaves people swimming or even drowning in a sea of moral, philosophical and intellectual relativism. There are no authorities to control us, no sure principles to guide us, no Bibles,

Qur'ans or other meta-narratives to dictate to us. No single truth stands as eternally valid and no virtue, other than tolerance, binds us in any way. In consequence, no spirituality, except an all-encompassing, syncretistic one, can restrict our lives and personal freedoms.

The challenges to Christians

The challenges to Christians in all of this are enormous. Here are several:

- The world is changing, so we have to be changing too, because we are approaching people who are struggling with change. But we must never change our Gospel message, as this is changeless, coming as it does from One who is "the same, yesterday, today and forever" (Hebrews 13:8).
- Because the world is suffering from information overload, our own message cannot just be information but has to be a message of demonstration and indeed transformation. People need to see that we are different and are practically and caringly engaged with them. The way of love takes on new importance and primacy.
- The world is facing choice overload. Therefore people to whom we would witness cannot be rushed into choosing Christ. A proper urgency of the Gospel must also make space for time and process in the matters of choice.
- Because the world is rushed, fatigued and burnt out, we must as Christian witnesses seek not to be rushed, fatigued and burnt out as well. It is hard to help such a world if we are indeed in that condition ourselves.
- We register that the world and those to whom we would witness are in deep pain, for many and various reasons. This is a major contact point for the Church and for all Christian believers, telling as we do of One who has "borne our griefs and carried our sorrows" (Isaiah 53:4) and who has also said, "come unto Me all you who labour and are heavy laden, and I will give you rest" (Matthew 11:28).

- Because the world is in such a mess relationally, the challenge to Christians is to witness, minister and demonstrate a world of good relationships at home, in the Church and in society. If we can demonstrate true connectedness and community, a lost and lonely world will feel a magnetic pull to our doors.
- Because the Postmodern world is sexually obsessed and sexually dissatisfied, we must as Christian witnesses and as the Church be ready to share the truths of biblical sexuality and convince a sceptical world that true sexual fulfilment is most truly found within the confines and principles of monogamous, heterosexual marriage.
- Because the world lives with Postmodern views of truth and morals as relative, variable and situational, we as Christian witnesses have to hold on uncompromisingly to the full deity and uniqueness of Jesus Christ, to biblical absolutes, to a firm moral code of some things right and others wrong and to the cornerstone of truth defined as, "coherence with the facts as they are." We would affirm that truth is universal and not local and that Truth is ultimately personal in Christ, rather than simply propositional in a statement. We would insist on holding to the law of antithesis that A is not non-A and that two contradictory statements cannot both be true at the same time.
- Above all we need to be caring people in a world crying out for care and we need to be loving people in a world that is very short on love. We must be willing to share our own stories and testimonies in such a way that they will attract rather than repel people in the Postmodern world around us. Our aim will be to demonstrate the truth of what we believe rather than simply trying to convince people by argument.

The Postmodern world out there is asking us, often with cries of anguish and also with real longing, whether we have anything that will really work for them. Have you something, each individual is saying, which will really work for me in my life? My relationships? My family? My sexuality? My mind? My body? My soul? My final future? The Christian answers that we do indeed have something that really works. But we need to show it. In reality we have Someone who really works. And if we can manifest Him credibly, the world will sit up in new ways to look at us, listen to us and then learn from us.

Hopefully the offerings of this volume will encourage readers to re-commit themselves afresh to our Lord Jesus Christ and then move out to the world in obedience not only to the Great Commandment to love but the Great Commission to share the Gospel with everyone. Jesus used His last earthly words to put this mandate upon us. Surely then His last words must be our first concern.

About the Author

Michael Cassidy is the founder and International Team Leader of African Enterprise, a ministry of evangelism, leadership development, reconciliation and aid and development which he launched in 1961 with the ultimate aim of *Evangelising the cities of Africa through word and deed in partnership with the Church.*

Cassidy was born in Johannesburg, grew up in Lesotho and completed his secondary education at Michaelhouse in KwaZulu-Natal. He became a Christian as a student at Cambridge University in England and received a call from God to city evangelism in Africa while participating in the 1957 Billy Graham Crusade in New York. This calling was further confirmed and refined during a summer vacation from his studies at Fuller Theological Seminary in California when, along with four fellow seminarians, he mounted an evangelistic mission to Pietermaritzburg in 1962.

The African Enterprise ministry has grown since then to encompass ministry teams in Congo (DRC), Ethiopia, Ghana, Kenya, Malawi, Rwanda, Tanzania, Uganda and Zimbabwe, as well as South Africa.

Cassidy has conducted evangelistic missions all across Africa and in many parts of the world. He has also spearheaded major gatherings of Christians in Africa over the past 32 years, beginning with the South African Congress on Mission and Evangelism in Durban in 1973, leading on to the Pan African Christian Leadership Assembly (PACLA) in Nairobi in 1976 and 1994, and the South African Christian Leadership Assembly (SACLA) in Pretoria in 1979 and 2003. He has also been involved extensively in reconciliation and peacemaking endeavours, most notably in behind-the-scenes initiatives that helped bring a peaceful transition to democracy in South Africa in 1994, which are chronicled in his book, *A Witness For Ever.*

Cassidy and his wife, Carol, live in Pietermaritzburg and have three children and four grandchildren.

For further information on the African Enterprise ministry, please contact:

African Enterprise
PO Box 13140 • Cascades • Pietermaritzburg 3202
• South Africa
+27-33-347-1911 phone • +27-33-347-1915 fax
aesa@africanenterprise.org.za
www.africanenterprise.org.za

Endnotes

1. *Protestant Christianity*, John Dillenberger and Claude Welch, Charles Scribner's Sons, New York, 1954, p. 178.
2. *What is Christianity?*, Adolf von Harnack, 2nd Edition, G.P. Putnam Sons, New York, 1901, pp. 25ff, quoted in *Fundamentalism and the Word of God*, James Packer, Inter-Varsity Press, Leicester, England, 1958, p. 149-150.
3. *The Interpretation of the Bible*, T.W. Manson, edited by C.W. Dugmore, SPCK, London, 1944, pp. 102ff.
4. *Christianity and Liberalism*, J. Gresham Machen, Victory Press, London, 1923, p. 7.
5. *Fundamentalism and the Word of God*, James Packer, Inter-Varsity Press, Leicester, England, 1958, p. 27.
6. *Evangelical Truth*, John R.W. Stott, Inter-Varsity Press, Leicester, England, 1999, p. 16.
7. *A Commentary on St Paul's Epistle to the Romans*, Martin Luther, James Clarke Publishers, 1953, p. 53.
8. *Works* of Hugh Latimer, Volume 1, pp. 30ff.
9. *Works* of John Jewell, Volume 2, p. 1034.
10. *The Character of a Methodist*, John Wesley, 1742, p. 10.
11. *The Evangelical Identity Problem*, an analysis by James Packer, Latimer House, Oxford, 1978, pp. 15-23. Alister McGrath expounds these six fundamentals or controlling principles in *Evangelisation and the Future of Christianity*, Hodder & Stoughton, London, 1994, pp. 49-88.
12. *Evangelisation in Modern Britain: A History from the 1930s to the 1980s*, D.W. Bebbington, Unwin Hyman, 1998, p. 3.
13. *A Passion for Truth – The Intellectual Coherence of Evangelicalism*, Alister McGrath, Apollos, an imprint of Inter-Varsity Press, Leicester, England, p. 22.

14. Op. cit., Stott, p. 28.
15. "The Phenomena of Scripture", Everett F. Harrison, in Symposium Volume, *Revelation and the Bible*, edited by Carl F.H. Henry, Baker Book House, Grand Rapids, Michigan, 1958, p. 239.
16. "Our Lord's Use of Scripture", Pierre Marcel in *Revelation and the Bible*, edited by Carl F.H. Henry, ibid., p. 207.
17. "The Church Doctrine of Inspiration", Geoffrey Bromiley, in *Revelation and the Bible*, ibid., p. 138.
18. *The Ante-Nicene Fathers*, First Epistle of Clement to the Corinthians, Charles Scribner's Sons, New York, 1899, Vol. 1, p. 19.
19. Epistle of Polycarp to the Philippians, VII.1, in *The Apostolic Fathers*, Vol. 1, William Heinemann, London and Harvard University Press, 1912, p. 293.
20. *Ante-Nicene Fathers*, Op. cit., Vol. 2, pp. 54, 56; also Vol. 1, pp. 414, 420, 440.
21. *The Case for Orthodox Theology*, Edward John Carnell, The Westminster Press, Philadelphia, 1959, p. 33.
22. *A Little Exercise for Young Theologians*, Helmut Thielicke, William B. Eerdmans, Grand Rapids, Michigan, 1962, p. 37.
23. *Fundamentalism and the Word of God*, James Packer, Inter-Varsity Press, Leicester, England, 1958, p. 47.
24. *Evangelical Truth*, John R.W. Stott, Inter-Varsity Press, Leicester, England, 1999, pp. 59-60..
25. Ibid., p. 60.
26. Ibid., p. 61.
27. *The Christian and His Bible*, Douglas Johnson, Inter-Varsity Press, London, 1953, p. 144.
28. *God in the Wasteland – The Reality of Truth in a World of Fading Dreams*, David F. Wells, William B. Eerdmans, Grand Rapids, Michigan, 1994, p. 150.
29. *Time of Crisis, Time to Confess*, Paul T. Stallsworth, Lutheran Forum 27, August 1993, p. 51.
30. *Anglican Essentials – Reclaiming Faith Within the Anglican Church of Canada*, George Egerton, editor, Barnabas Anglican Ministries, Toronto, 1995, p. 74. See essay: "On Track With the Word of God" by Peter Mason.

31. Ibid., p. 74.
32. Ibid., p. 74.
33. *The Ante-Nicene Fathers*, Charles Scribner's Sons, New York, 1899, Vol. 2, pp. 79-80.
34. Ibid., pp. 93-96.
35. Ibid., pp. 140ff.
36. *The Knowledge of God in Calvin's Theology*, Edward Downey, Jr Columbia Publishing House, New York, 1952, p. 91. For Calvin's overall posture, see *Institutes of the Christian Religion*, edited by John Baillie, Henry van Dusen, John T. McNeill, Westminster Press, Philadelphia, 1960, John Calvin, Vol. 1, chap. 7, sections 1-5 (pp. 74-81). Also chap. 8, pp. 81ff and chap. 9, pp. 93ff.
37. *Briefwechsel*, Enders and Kaweran, editors, I, 141 – and quoted in "The Church Doctrine of Inspiration" by Geoffrey Bromiley, in Symposium Volume, *Revelation and the Bible*, edited by Carl F.H. Henry, Baker Book House, Grand Rapids, Michigan, 1958, pp. 211-212.
38. *Parker Society*, edited, p. 296. Quoted in Bromiley, ibid., (see note 5), p. 212.
39. *Protestant Christianity*, John Dillenberger and Claude Welch, Charles Scribner's Sons, New York, 1954, p. 223.
40. "Modern Theology and Biblical Criticism", C.S. Lewis, essay in *Christian Reflections – A Collection of Fourteen Papers*, William B. Eerdmans, Grand Rapids, Michigan, 1967. See pp. 152-166 for the full exposition of this posture.
41. Ibid.
42. *The Case for Orthodox Theology*, Edward John Carnell, The Westminster Press, Philadelphia, 1959, p. 53.
43. Ibid., see chap. 4, pp. 51-65.
44. Quoted in *C.S. Lewis, Mere Christian*, Kathryn Ann Lindskog, Regal Press, Glendale, California, 1973, frontispiece to p. 1. See also her biographical note #1 on p. 16.
45. *Christian Reflections*, C.S. Lewis, William B. Eerdmans, Grand Rapids, Michigan, 1967, p. 152.
46. *God in the Dock*, C.S. Lewis, William B. Eerdmans, Grand Rapids, Michigan, 1970, p. 181.

47. *The Grand Miracle*, C.S. Lewis, Ballantine Books, New York, 1986, p. 75.
48. *Mere Christianity*, C.S. Lewis, Macmillan Publishing, New York, 1977, pp. 54-56.
49. Ibid., p. 189.
50. Ibid., p. 190.
51. If you are not very well acquainted with the life, thought and work of C.S. Lewis, you may like to start with *Mere Christianity, The Screwtape Letters*, or *The Problem of Pain*. Good biographies are by George Sayer – *Jack: A Life of C.S. Lewis*, published by Hodder & Stoughton – and by A.N. Wilson – *C.S. Lewis: A Biography*, published by HarperCollins. Also, if you have children, try *The Lion, the Witch and the Wardrobe* as well as other books from *The Chronicles of Narnia* series and start them early on a magical and spiritually scintillating adventure. The movie *Shadowlands* tells the great love story of Lewis' relationship with Joy Davidman, but have your handkerchief ready when you watch it!
52. *The Joyful Christian*, C.S. Lewis, Charles Scribner's Sons, New York, 1996, p. 125.
53. *The Jesus I Never Knew*, Philip Yancey, Marshall Pickering, London, 1995, p. 23. See also Yancey's whole chap. 1, pp. 11-23.
54. *Countdown – A Time to Choose*, G.B. Handy, Moody Press, Chicago, 1961, p. 33.
55. Quoted in *Basic Christianity*, John R.W. Stott, Inter-Varsity Press, Leicester, England, 1958, p. 47.
56. Quoted in *Evidence That Demands a Verdict*, Josh McDowell, Campus Crusade for Christ, Inc., San Bernardino, California, 1972, p. 201.
57. *How Modern Should Theology Be?*, Helmut Thielicke, Collins Fontana Books, London & Glasgow, 1970, p. 18.
58. Ibid., p. 19.
59. Ibid., p. 20.
60. *Theological Dictionary of the New Testament*, edited by Gerhard Kittel and Gerhard Friedrich, translated by Geoffrey Bromiley, abridged in one volume, William B Eerdmans, Grand Rapids, Michigan, 1985, p. 772.

61. *The Cross of Christ*, John R.W. Stott, Inter-Varsity Press, Leicester, England, 1986, p. 160.
62. *Prisoners of Hope*, Michael Cassidy, African Enterprise, Pietermaritzburg, 1974, p. 116.
63. *Bursting the Wineskins*, Michael Cassidy, Hodder & Stoughton, London, 1983.
64. *How to Be Filled With the Holy Spirit*, A.W. Tozer, Christian Publications, Inc., Harrisburg, Pennsylvania.
65. *Systematic Theology*, a compendium by Augustus Hopkins Strong, The Judson Press, Philadelphia, 1907, p. 869.
66. *The Catholic Faith*, W.H. Griffith Thomas, Church Book Room Press, Ltd., London, 1960, p. 63.
67. My own listing of the primary giftings are as follows, drawn also from *Bursting the Wineskins*, Michael Cassidy, Hodder & Stoughton, London, 1983, pp.282-283: **Ministry Gifts:** *Apostles, Prophets, Evangelists, Pastors, Teachers* – Acts 6:4, 21:8; Romans 12:7; 1 Corinthians 12:28; Ephesians 4:11,12; Colossians 4:17; 1 Timothy 1:12; 2 Timothy 4:5, 11. **Knowledge Gifts:** *Word of Wisdom* – 1 Corinthians 12:8; *Word of Knowledge* – 1 Corinthians 12:8. **Gifts of Power:** *Faith* – 1 Corinthians 12:9, (Acts 13:16); *Healing* – 1 Corinthians 12:9, 28; *Working of Miracles* – 1 Corinthians 12:10, 28, 29; *Discerning of Spirits* – 1 Corinthians 12:10. **Gifts of Utterance (Saying):** *Prophecy* – Acts 2:17, 18, 19:6, 21:19; Romans 12:6; 1 Corinthians 11:4, 5, 12:10, 13:2, 8, 9, 14:1, 3, 4, 5, 6, 22, 24, 31, 39; 1 Timothy 1:18, 4:14; *Diverse Kinds of Tongues* – Mark 16:17; Acts 2:4, 11, 10:46, 19:6; 1 Corinthians 12:10, 28, 30, 13:1, 8, 14:2, 4, 5, 6, 13, 14, 18, 19, 22, 23, 26, 27, 39; *Interpretation of Tongues* – 1 Corinthians 12:10, 30, 14:5, 13, 26, 27, 28. **Other Gifts:** *Helps* – 1 Corinthians 12:28; *Administration* – 1 Corinthians 12:28; *Service* – Romans 12:7; 2 Corinthians 8:4, 9:1; 1 Peter 4:11; *Exhortation* – Acts 13:15; Romans 12:8; 1 Corinthians 14:3; 1 Timothy 4:13; Hebrews 13:22; *Giving* – Romans 12:8; 2 Corinthians 9:7; Philippians 4:15; *Leading* – Romans 12:8; Hebrews 13:7, 17, 24; 1 Timothy 5:17; *Showing Mercy* – Romans 12:8; *Revelation* – 1 Corinthians 14:6, 26; 2 Corinthians 12:1, 7; Galatians 2:2.
68. An effective and helpful study of the spiritual gifts comes in C.

Peter Wagner's book *Your Spiritual Gifts Can Help Your Church Grow*, Regal Books, Glendale, California, 1979. See also for Wagner's more comprehensive list of spiritual gifts in my book *Bursting the Wineskins*, pp.278-79.
69. Op. cit., Strong, p. 873.
70. "The Christian Apologist", Austen Farrer, in *Light on C.S. Lewis*, ed. Jocelyn Gibb, Harcourt & Brace, New York, 1965, p. 26.
71. Ibid., p. 29.
72. *Compelling Reason*, C.S. Lewis, Fount, London, 1996, p. 69.
73. Ibid., p. 67.
74. Ibid., p. 64-65.
75. Ibid., p. 79.
76. *The Problem of Pain*, C.S. Lewis, Macmillan, New York, 1948, p. 115.
77. *Miracles: A Preliminary Study*, C.S. Lewis, Collins Fontana Books, 1947, pp. 9ff.
78. *The Abolition of Man*, C.S. Lewis, Found, London, 1973, p. 19. See chapter entitled "Men Without Chests".
79. Ibid., p. 19.
80. Ibid., pp. 19-20.
81. *The Great Divorce*, C.S. Lewis, Touchstone, New York, 1996, p. 40.
82. Ibid., pp. 41-42.
83. Ibid., p. 9.
84. Ibid., p. 10.
85. Op. cit., *The Abolition of Man*, p. 16.
86. Ibid., p. 29.
87. Ibid., pp. 39-40.
88. *Mere Christianity*, C.S. Lewis, Macmillan, New York, 1977, p. 19.
89. Ibid., p. 21.
90. I am indebted to John Stott for the notion of three types of tolerance – legal, social and intellectual.
91. *One Road Only*, David Hewetson, Anglican Information Office, Sydney, 1980, pp. 9-10, italics his.
92. Ibid., p. 10, italics his.
93. *Nature, Man and God*, William Temple, Macmillan, New York,

1964. See final chapter: "The Hunger of Natural Revelation", pp. 490-520.
94. Ibid., pp. 12-13.
95. *The Shelter of Each Other*, Mary Pipher, Ballantine Books, New York, 1996, p. 81.
96. *Transforming Mission*, David J. Bosch, Orbis Books, Maryknoll, New York, 1993, p. 267.
97. *Believing in the Future*, David J. Bosch, Trinity Press International, Valley Forge, Pennsylvania, 1995, p. 5.
98. Op. cit., *Transforming Mission*, p. 267.
99. Op. cit., *Believing in the Future*, p. 13.
100. Essay by James Hunter in *Faith and Modernity*, edited by Philip Sampson, Vinay Samuel, Chris Sugden, Regnum Books, Oxford, 1994, p. 17.
101. *A Passion for Truth*, Alister McGrath, Apollos, an imprint of Inter-Varsity Press, Leicester, 1996, p. 164.
102. *Fit Bodies, Fat Minds*, Os Guinness, Hodder & Stoughton, London, 1994, p. 105.
103. *A Primer on Postmodernism*, Stanley J. Grenz, William B. Eerdmans, Grand Rapids, Michigan, 1996, p. 13.
104. Ibid., p. 13.
105. Ibid., pp. 13-14.
106. *The Contemporary Christian*, John R.W. Stott, Inter-Varsity Press, Leicester, England, 1992, p. 296.
107. Quoted in *Turning Points*, Vaughan Roberts, Operation Mobilisation, Carlyle, England, 1998, p. 73.
108. The name and identity of the magazine where this quote was originally located is now unknown to the author.

Index

Aaron (brother of Moses) 117
Abraham (Hebrew Patriarch) 73, 79, 119
Adam 82
America (United States) 19, 20, 21, 40, 49
Anglican Church 27
Anselm 27
Apocrypha 16
Apologetics 122-132
Apostles' Creed 15, 27
Aquinas, Thomas 27, 48
Athanasius 15, 16, 46-47
Augsburg Confession 27
Augustine 15, 27, 47, 78, 119, 153
Barth, Karl 14, 51, 52
Bebbington, David 26
Beethoven, Ludwig von 33
Belgium 51
Bohemia 17
Book of Common Prayer (Anglican) 65, 92
Bosch, David 153, 154-155
Buddha, Buddhist, Buddhism 79, 142, 146, 161
Bultmann, Rudolph 51, 53
Bunyan, John 119, 121
Calvin, John 17, 20, 27, 48
Cambridge, England 64, 94
Carnell, Edward John 35, 58
Canon (of Scripture) 15
Chalcedon, credal statement of 15
Chambers, Oswald 115

Charismatic .... see Pentecostal
Clarke, Sir Edward 76
Clement of Alexandria 15, 27, 35, 46
Confucius 79
Constantine (Emperor) 152
Copernicus 49
Council of Trent 49
Cranmer, Thomas 64-65
Cullman, Oscar 51, 52
Cyprian 15, 46
Darling, Lord 78
David (King of Israel) 73
Dillenberger, John 19-20, 51
Drake, Sir Francis 114
Egypt 87
England 17, 19, 48, 65
Enlightenment 19, 27, 40, 49-50, 55, 154-156, 158, 159, 160
Europe 19, 50, 154
Evangelical, Evangelicalism 13, 24, 25, 27, 28, 30, 33, 54, 55, 65, 107-108
Farrer, Austen 124
Fide sola 17
Florence, Italy 17
Footner, Robert 94
Ford, Leighton 104-105
France 40, 49
Franks, Lynne 160
Fundamentalist, Fundamentalism 13, 21, 22, 23, 24, 25, 29
Galileo Galilei 49, 154
Geneva, Switzerland 17
Germany 17, 19, 48
Graham, Billy 97-98, 104, 167
Great Awakening 19
Gregory I (Pope) 16
Grenz, Stanley 159-160, 162
Griffith Thomas, W.H. 116

Guinness, Os	158-159
Harnack, Adolph von	20, 51
Henley, W.E.	149
Hermeneutics, Hermeneutical	55, 57, 63
Hewetson, David	10, 144-145, 146
Holy Spirit, Spirit of God	36, 38, 41, 46, 47, 48, 49, 59, 61, 63, 74, 94, 96, 98, 100, 105, 106-113, 114, 115, 117, 118, 120, 121, 122, 124, 131-132, 133
Hooper, Walter	66
Humanism, Humanistic	21, 51
Hunter, James	156
Hus, Jan	17
Indulgences	17
Irenaeus	15, 35, 46
Islam, Muslim, Muslims	24, 129, 146, 162
James (Apostle)	61
Jesus Christ	9, 14, 30, 31, 32, 34, 36, 37, 38, 41, 42, 43, 44, 45, 46, 50, 51, 52, 58, 59, 60, 61, 64, 66, 67-71, 72-80, 81, 83-84, 85-93, 94-95, 99, 101-102, 103-105, 106, 108, 109-113, 115, 116, 117, 119, 120, 121, 122, 128, 130-132, 133, 139-141, 143, 144, 145, 147, 152-153, 155, 156, 161-162, 164, 165-166
Jewel, John	25
John (Apostle)	34, 35, 74-75, 76, 92, 101
Johnson, Douglas	40
Joseph (Father of Jesus)	73-74
Judas Iscariot	76
Justin Martyr	15
Kaiser Wilhelm II	51

Kennedy, Studdert 118
Kerygma 54
Knox, John 27
Latimer, Bishop Hugh 25, 65
Lazarus (friend of Jesus) 75
Lewis, C.S. 53, 54, 63, 64, 65, 66-70,
 72, 122-126, 129-132, 133-
 141, 146, 162
Liberal, Liberalism 13, 19, 20, 21, 24, 28, 29,
 40, 50, 51, 52, 136
Louvain, Belgium 51
Luke (author of Luke and Acts) 34, 73
Luther, Martin 17, 20, 25, 27, 48, 153
Lutheran Church 27
Machen, J. Gresham 21
Manson, T.W. 20-21
Mark (author of Gospel of Mark) 75
Marx, Karl 160
Mary (Mother of Jesus) 74
Mason, Peter 44
McGrath, Alister 26, 158, 162
Methodist, Methodism 19
Middle Ages 16, 17, 47, 48, 53
Mill, John Stuart 29
Modern, Modernity 41, 42, 53, 79-80, 136, 151,
 155-157, 158, 159
Moravia, Moravian 18, 19
Moses 32, 58, 79, 82, 117
Muhammad 79, 129
Muslim, Muslims .... see Islam
Naturalism, Naturalistic 53, 66, 79, 130
Nebuchadnezzar 66
Neill, Bishop Stephen 102
Neuhaus, Richard John 140
Nicene Creed 15, 27, 109
Nietzsche, Friedrich 156
Ninety-Five Theses (Luther) 17

Origen	15, 27, 46
Oxford, England	64, 65
Packer, James I.	21, 25, 37, 134-136
Palestine	60
Paul (Apostle)	14, 33, 34, 35, 38, 43, 52, 55, 59, 60, 61, 70, 75, 78, 80, 83-84, 87, 89-91, 95, 101, 109, 111, 114, 115, 116, 117, 118, 120, 128, 139-140, 143, 145
Pentecostal, Pentecostalism, Charismatic	54, 106, 107, 108, 112
Peter (Apostle)	34, 55, 77, 88, 91-92, 96, 101-102, 122
Pietism, Pietists	18, 19, 20
Pilgrim Fathers	19
Pipher, Mary	150
Plato	134
Pluralism	142-147
Polycarp	27, 35, 46
Postmodern, Postmodernism	9, 40, 41, 67, 79, 123, 127, 147, 148-166
Presbyterian Church	27, 39
Purgatory	17
Puritans, Puritanism	19, 20
Reformation	17, 18, 48
Reformers	17, 18, 25, 40, 42, 48, 49, 53, 62
Ridley, Bishop Nicholas	65
Roman Catholic Church	16, 49
Roman Empire	16, 151-152
Rowan, Peter	150
Salvation	17
Savonarola, Girolamo	17
Schaeffer, Francis	130
Schleiermacher, Friedrich	19, 50
Scholasticism	18

Social Gospel ... 20
Sola scriptura ... 17
Solomon ... 58
South Africa ... 23
Stalin, Josef ... 157
Stallsworth, Paul T. ... 41
Star Wars ... 157
Stott, John ... 25, 26, 38-39, 88, 143, 160
Strong, Augustus ... 114, 118-119
Switzerland ... 48
Temple, William ... 27, 144, 145
Tertullian ... 15, 27, 46
Thielicke, Helmut ... 35, 79-80
Thirty-Nine Articles ... 27, 49, 109
Thomas à Kempis ... 120
Timothy (disciple of Apostle Paul) ... 14, 38, 114
Tolerance ... 9, 142-145, 161, 164
Tozer, A.W. ... 112
Troeltsch, Ernest ... 51
Turney, Jane ... 160-161
Tyndale, William ... 17
Vancouver, Canada ... 159
Vulgate ... 17
Welch, Claude ... 19-20, 51
Wells, David ... 41
Wesley, John ... 18, 20, 25, 27
Westminster Catechism ... 39
Westminster Confession ... 27
Willard, Dallas ... 126-128
Wittenberg, Germany ... 17
World War I ... 51
Wycliffe, John ... 17, 25
Yancey, Philip ... 72
Zinzendorf, Nicholas Ludwig von ... 18
Zurich, Switzerland ... 17
Zwingli, Ulrich ... 17, 48